Dave
from
Frank + Trudie

Christmas 1966

The New England Year

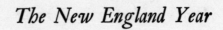

Also by Haydn S. Pearson

NEW ENGLAND FLAVOR

COUNTRY FLAVOR COOKBOOK

HAYDN S. PEARSON

The New England Year

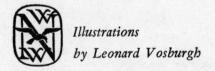

Illustrations
by Leonard Vosburgh

W · W · NORTON & COMPANY · INC · NEW YORK

To the memory of Father,
who taught me some of the meanings of a New England year.

Foreword

What is a New England year?

It is a symphony in four major movements as nature's orchestra matches the moods of the seasons. In this book I have tried to describe the natural sequence of the seasons. Many of us look but do not see; we listen but do not hear.

New England is unique in its climate and topography. There are rocky shore lines where the waves beat bass drums; there are fertile river meadows where gentle breezes ripple grass waves and the music is like distant flutes. There are craggy mountains where winter blizzards bring a sound like the wailing of oboes. There are rock-studded pasture hillsides where the wind among scraggly pasture oaks reminds one of distant organ music.

New England's rivers rush down from the highlands. A century and more ago water-powered mills in the valleys called boys and girls from thin-soiled upland farms. Part of the year's symphony is the melody of brooks that sing down from granite-edged uplands and join forces to form our rivers.

I am also writing of my boyhood days in Hancock, New Hampshire, where Father was a minister-farmer. For many years he preached in the beautiful white, tall-steepled church facing the village common. We lived on a 120-acre general farm. We had cows, horses, hens, and pigs, but Father's special interest was the 800-tree Baldwin apple orchard.

In this six-state area, our activities are determined by the seasons. I learned the year's farming activities. I know what it is to plow and harrow in rocky soil. I have hoed and cultivated farm crops and helped harvest the hay. I have worked in the woods in winter and hauled loads of logs to the mill.

In 1908, when we came to the farm, we did not have a telephone, electric lights, or radio. I watched these boons to rural living come in the following years. We had snow rollers to pack down the roads in the winter; we used horse-drawn scrapers to get the roads in shape after mud time.

It is my hope that this book will combine a picture of the activities of country-living half a century ago with a feeling for nature's beauty. And I hope that when you have finished the book, the harvest will be some of the truths that have given man faith as he travels through the years.

HAYDN S. PEARSON

Sunny Acres
Greenfield, N.H.

Contents

FOREWORD   7

JANUARY: *A Trip to the Village. Winter Birds. Ice–Cutting Time. Making Sausage. Places of the Past. January Snow. Snow Rolling. Working in the Woods. Woodsheds. The Mail-Order List. Winter Silence. First–Month Moon.*   15

FEBRUARY: *Trust the Ground Hog. One Special Day. February Walk. A Boy's Winter Day. Farm Shop. Pleasures of the Parlor. Saturday Night Bath. Sleigh Riding. February Moonlight.*   37

MARCH: *Geranium in the Window. Barn Doorway. Setting Hen. The Miracles of March. March Birds. Cake Era. Working Up the Wood. Woodboxes. Housecleaning. Apple Trees. Picking–Over Time. Night Boiling.*   59

APRIL: *Spring Tonic. April Woodland. April Rain. Annual Horse Auction. April Tasks. Plowing. Sounds of Spring. Horse–Hair Time. Pie and Biscuits. Parsnips. Moving Out the Stove.*   81

MAY: *The Pipes of Pan. May Flowers. Building Character. Kitchen Marvels. Woodland Brook. Fishing. Meadow Music Makers. Hedgerows.*   103

JUNE: *Wild Strawberries. One Woodland Hour. Marching Evergreens. Old Swimming Hole. The Golden Grains. Wooden Watering Troughs. Meadow Music. Weeding. First Mess of Peas. The Flowers of June.*   123

JULY: *Picking Potato Bugs. Berries. Rain on the Roof. A Tree That Stands Alone. Cherries. Springhouse. Haying. Tin Peddler. The Rooster. Horseradish. Sir Christopher Wren. Fourth of July. July Evening.*   141

AUGUST: *Green Apples. Woodland Waterfall. R.F.D. Getting the Cows. Ladder and Basket Man. The Golden Tinge. August Flowers. Bee Lining. Aerial Circus. Teaching Pullets to Roost. Hammocks. August Evening.*   161

SEPTEMBER: *The Simple and Straightforward. Stacking Beans. Picklin' Time. Debating, Sermonizing and Milking. Old Iron Kettles. Line Storm. Nature's Own. Picking Apples. The Fiddlers. Farm Evenings Long Ago. First Fire. First Frost Tonight.*   183

OCTOBER: *Autumn Voices. October Glory. Water Witch. Saturday Chores. Country Lane. The Skunk That Couldn't. The Fringe-Top Surrey. Ingathering Time. Foretelling Winter Weather.*   201

NOVEMBER: *Indian Summer. Woodland Ravine. Stump-Sitting. Autumn Pies. Making Land. Barn Chores. The Sleepers. Smoke from Farm Chimneys. Extended Architecture. Lighting-Up Time. Mother and the Model T. Buttoning Up. Rising Wind.*   221

DECEMBER: *The First Snowfall. The Chickadee. Skating Party. Flailing Beans. One-Hole Corn Sheller. Train Whistle. The Lamplighter. Saturday Night Trading. The White Lady. Kindling for Winter. Kitchen Rocking Chair. Feather Beds. December Sunset. Christmas.*   241

The New England Year

JANUARY

JANUARY IS THE HEART OF WINTER, AND THE EARTH IS HARD and cold. This is the month of the Lean-Wolf Moon. Foxes make their solitary rounds and deer browse in evergreen swamps. Birds come around the feeders, and at night barred owls hoot from the woodland. After a fresh fall of snow, there are stories to be read in the whiteness: footprints of field mice, tracks of pheasants, and perhaps a few congealed bits of scarlet blood where an owl has pounced on a rabbit.

There are spells of zero cold; there are blizzards that cry in the night. January brings days when the wind whimpers in the chimney. But the first month also has bright, sparkling days when a thin gold sun rides across the sky. A blanket of snow covers northland hills; it has been tucked tightly into winding river valleys and draped snugly over upland ridges and pasture knolls. On a windless, cold, clear January day it seems as if time were standing still and as if all of nature's activities had come to a halt. One who does not appreciate the facts might say, "This is a time of balance. The scales have no motion."

But to the man who has both knowledge and wisdom, certain basic truths are clear. Each month of the turning year brings profound changes, and each segment of the annual cycle means fundamental progress in the ever-ceasing evolution of life-giving forces on our planet. The January countryside seems starkly simple, but beneath the apparent calm, there is always movement.

On the windswept heights, bits of frozen moisture, plus tugging air currents, loosen small bits of rock with their basic chemicals, and the life-giving elements for plant nourishment start their long journey to the lowlands. Beneath the snow that covers fields and meadows, bleached, lifeless grasses are breaking down; alternate cold and warmth hasten the process. In the woodlands, among the hardwood and evergreens, the lower layer of spongy soil carpet is readying to change to vital humus. The accumulated weight of ice and snow exerts powerful pressure. Winter rains and sleet, winds that break trunks and branches, frozen water that expands in craggy rocks and in hollow trunks are integral parts of a natural process that has been continuing for many millions of years.

A Trip to the Village

Can you hear them? Hear those high, sweet notes floating overhead? Hear the jangle of the rhythmic tolling bells? That melody is the winter music of yesteryear, music made before rubber tires displaced steel runners that squeaked and crunched on hard-packed snow.

A farm family could tell who was going to town by the music of the bells. Some farmers preferred bells on the shafts of pung or sleigh; some preferred the body straps with fifteen or more bells. Work horses had single large bells attached to their collars. As the big teams swung along the two-track road, their pace was reflected in the musical notes that carried far in cold, clear, winter air.

The Swiss Shaft Chimes on the pung—two iron straps with four bells of graduated sizes on each strap—made pleasant music as the Morgan mare whisked a boy to town to get a couple of bags of cottonseed meal. The Harmonized Swiss Pole Chimes on the high-backed, single-seat sleigh were more satisfying because there were six bells on each strap, and, as the mail-order catalog said, the bells were "harmonized by an expert."

When I was a boy, the bells on the work horses in winter were used on the cows in the summer time. Some farmers liked the sweet-toned bells that sounded like the tolled notes of the village church clock. Other farmers preferred the harsh, hollow notes made by pressed metal. But even the metallic clangings seemed to have a musical quality when heard from a distance on a calm winter's day.

Winter Birds

A nature lover sometimes wonders at the scientific names attached to birds. The sprightly, hustling little downy woodpecker has a mouth-filling tag: *Dryobates pubescens medianus*. This smallest of all our woodpeckers is a good example of patience, perseverance, and cheerfulness. Sometimes one wonders how this and other small birds survive below-zero spells. The downy, like the chickadee, finds deep holes in decayed trunks or branches and seeks sanctuary when the weather is bitter.

The downy is not so popular as the chickadee, but it is a welcome visitor around the farm and is grateful for the suet that is provided. It is a plain-colored bird, gray, black, and white, although the male has a scarlet band on his head. Most of us take the downy for granted, but it is one of our most interesting birds. Its foot, for example, has an unusual physical feature, one of nature's miracles of adaptation. Instead of three toes in front and one in back, as with most birds, the downy has two in front and two in back. Watch the downy as it clings to a tree, and you will see how the wide-spread hind claws brace the bird in a wind and prevent sidesway. The downy's tail has stiff spines to help brace against the tree; its long tongue has a horny-backed tip with which to extract grubs and larvae from wood or bark.

Come spring the downies make their nests in hollow limbs or trunks, and the entrance is usually barely large enough for the parents to go through. When the chicks are ten to twelve days old, they make a tremendous chattering as the parents arrive with food. The little downy is not spectacular, and its few nasal notes cannot be called music. But he is a steady-going fellow who is industrious and minds his own business.

The blue jay is a noisy, aggressive citizen—a common thief, both cunning and bold. Like the crow, the jay takes toll each year of other birds' eggs and nestlings. A man feels his blood pressure rise when frantic robins suddenly sound a wild alarm on a beautiful June day and he sees a jay leave the lilac bush where the robins have built their nest. But one should never forget that each species of animal life lives according to instinct passed down through the centuries.

On a sparkling, cold winter's day, when there is white beauty on the hills, the blue jays flash among the old apple trees behind the barn; they come to the bird feeders and snatch chunks of suet. Jays are highly intelligent birds—ranking with the crow in this respect. They cache nuts in the fall, and no one knows how many great trees a century hence will be the result of the jays' activities during autumn weeks. Thoreau wrote of their call, "The unrelenting steel-cold scream of a jay, that never flows into a song, a sort of wintry trumpet, screaming cold, hard, tense frozen music, like the winter sky itself."

Blue jays on a brittle-cold winter day are an integral part of the spirit of winter. The raucous, aggressive screams remind the countryman of a pulsing north wind; the flash of blue resembles the color of the January sky on a cloudless day. And while blue jays, like men, emphasize their bad qualities with unnecessary display, they also, like most human beings, have qualities that give them a place in this contrary world.

Ice-Cutting Time

When a boy was twelve years old or thereabouts, it was perfectly logical that he have two opinions about the annual ice harvest. If you were brought up on a farm in the northland back in the days of iceboxes instead of electric refrigerators, you can probably guess what I mean. Ice-cutting was hard, cold work. But when a fellow thought of June, July, and August, and the six-quart White Mountain ice cream freezer, he realized there had to be ice before he could enjoy ice cream.

Farmers kept an eye on the *Old Farmer's Almanac* and on the weather as the new year came in. There was an occasional year when December was a cold month with below-zero temperatures, and the ice harvest was completed in December. But on the average, ice-cutting time did not come until well into January. Farmers wanted ice that was ten to twelve inches thick. They hoped for good clear ice that was not mixed with sleet or snow.

When conditions were right, it was a rushing time for a few days, and everyone hoped that the weather would hold. This was one of the few times when we boys were allowed to miss school. Teacher understood, and there was never any difficulty. She always said we could "make up" the work, but so far as I remember, we simply went on from where we left off.

It may be that International Falls, out west somewhere, is the coldest spot in the United States, but if I were asked to name it, I would say that Norway Pond in Hancock village deserves the honor. You just don't know what cold is until you work on a pond at zero or below with a stiff wind blowing from the northwest. It didn't help our morale to hear farmers joke about us. "One place where we can get an honest day's work from the boys," they said. "They've either got to work or freeze to death."

It was well-organized effort. If snow were on the ice, the snow was cleared off first. We put a plank at an angle through the front runners of the two horse sleds, and working the same way, shoved the snow to one side. This is the same technique that the snow plows use on roads.

When the area was cleared, it was "plowed." This means that a plow with a sharp steel vertical blade cut a slit in the ice to a depth of two to four inches. A marker attached to the plow insured that each line would be parallel to the next. This meant uniform-sized cakes after the area was plowed each way.

Then came the sawing—the part that we boys disliked most of all. An ice saw is four feet long and has a curved metal strip at the large end. To this curved metal strip a crossbar is attached. The procedure was to put a hand on each side of the crossbar, bend over a bit, and push the saw up and down in the slit cut by the plow. That's all there is to sawing out the ice. But it doesn't say anything about aching backs and shoulder muscles. It doesn't say how the cold wind cut through a mackinaw, wool shirt, and woolen union suit. You must saw ice under wintry conditions to know what it means.

The rest of the process was not too bad. After the cakes were cut, we pushed them through a channel of crackling, icy, black-looking water to the shore of the pond. As soon as the ice was out in the cold air, the cakes dried. Hauling it home was the pleasant part of the whole business. We put two layers of the cakes on the sled. It was heavy but on hard-packed sled tracks, almost icy smooth, Old Jerry and Charlie, our farm horses, had no trouble. On very cold, windy days, boys walked behind the sled swinging their arms to stir up circulation.

At the farm, the horses drew up in front of the icehouse, and cake by cake we pushed the heavy, oblong, gray-green cakes up an oak plank. As the layers grew higher, it was a trick to keep the ice block on the smooth, slippery plank. Layer by layer the house was filled. Around the sides we left a space approximately a foot wide. Sawdust was shovelled into this space, and my job was to tamp it down thoroughly with a four-by-four piece of wood. "Don't be easy on the job," Father said. "If you tamp the sawdust tight, it means we won't lose so much from melting in hot weather."

At the end of three or four days, we had our three hundred cakes safely harvested. They were in good level layers, with a smattering of sawdust between the layers, to a generous depth over the top.

I have handled hundreds, yes, thousands of cakes of ice. I don't want to handle any more. But it would be sort of fun on a hot summer's day to go once more to that old icehouse on the farm and haul out a sawdust-covered cake to freeze a batch of Mother's rich, smooth ice cream.

Making Sausage

When steady winter cold had settled in, and hills and fields were white with the snow that farmers hoped would last through sugaring, there came the annual butchering time. After the meat was cut and trimmed, hams and bacon prepared for pickling, and the chunks of fat pork readied for the big brine barrel beneath the cellar stairs, Mother got at the sausage-making.

There was something about sausage-making that kept a

young man close to the kitchen—the anticipation of those patties Mother fried up to see if the seasoning was right. The old recipe for meat proportions was easy to follow; it had been handed down through generations: three parts fresh lean meat and one part fat. I was glad to turn the grinder and watch the ground meat come oozing through the holes. The mechanical part was easy.

But when it was time to determine just exactly the right amount of seasoning, advice was welcome. Everybody offered his own opinion, and, of course, the only way to tell whether the sage, nutmeg, ginger, marjoram, black pepper and salt were in the right proportions was to fry a few small cakes. Then that wonderful saliva-starting, nostril-tickling aroma filled the kitchen, spread through the summer kitchen, and out into the woodshed. There is no smell quite like it, even though some solid citizens insist frying bacon has a better fragrance.

Naturally the seasoning is never quite right the first time, and a willing lad spent a few minutes cutting kindling while the sausage was reworked. In a little while a new sample was ready to be tasted. That was one of the satisfying things about sausage-making. It required several samplings before it was ready to be stuffed into the cloth casings.

Places of the Past

Nowadays all the dusty stalls are empty, and in the far corner of the barn the old harness room is quiet and cobwebs mat dust-covered windows. Dried and brittle harnesses hang from oaken pegs. The can of dressing on the shelf still has a bit of the black material that shined the leather long ago after the harness was washed. The younger generation would not recognize such names as hame, lazy strap, belly band, crupper, check rein, choke strap, blind, throat latch, winker stay, bag swivel, and crown piece.

The harness room drowses through the years. Harnesses hang from their pegs, reminders of an era that is gone. Gray stable blankets, and the colorful blankets which covered the horses in the winter when we went to the village, are reminders of the time when ten miles an hour was rapid traveling. When someone walks into the old harness room, he smells a faint, heady aroma. Harnesses no longer shine with good care. Horses that were once friends are gone, but memories flood back.

Old barns are friendly buildings—if a man knew one in his boyhood. Perhaps most memorable of all was the smell of the barn, a smell compounded of hay and grain, livestock, sawdust, manure, and the leather of the harness room. There was a feeling of peace and security among sleek horses and placid cows. Since barns were first built, boys have jumped from high scaffolds to piles of hay on the floor, and then dared their sisters to do the same. They have dug tunnels along the sides of the heaped mows and hunted the scaffolds for nests where free-ranging hens laid their eggs. Of course, there were chores in the barns, too—cows to milk, calves to feed, cleaning to be done, and bedding to be spread.

Old barns are a meaningful part of the history and tradition of our country. Weather-stained and gray, with sagging roof lines, leaning out of plumb, with gaping windows and doors ajar from broken hinges, they are as much a part of the countryside as covered bridges. Old weathered barns are disappearing as farms on back roads are being abandoned. New barns are more compact and scientifically designed to save footsteps, but the old barns were solidly built, and some will serve for a long time to come, memorials to an era that is gone.

Blacksmiths' shops and livery stables are things of the past, too. I am about ready to concede that horseless carriages are here to stay; but I still believe that a good-stepping horse takes a man through life as fast as is safe and necessary. Besides, the social order functioned better when we had blacksmiths' shops.

Granted, the shop wasn't much to look at, just a weathered, low building with a pile of cultch heaped high outside the door. Inside, it was dark and dingy. Windows were gray-streaked and covered with tangled masses of dark cobwebs. The floor was grimy and littered with hoof parings, bits of metal, and debris. At one end was a heap of cultivators, plows, and other farm tools waiting for repairs; for the old-time smith was also a general repair man. On the stringers overhead were long lines of new horseshoes, massive, heavy shoes for the big farm teams, and light, dainty shoes for fast roaders.

It was always a good day when Father said after breakfast, "Son, better take Old Jerry to town and get new shoes." It was interesting to watch the smith work the bellows and heat a shoe red hot in the glowing coals. He put the shoe on the anvil and pounded it to the right shape to fit the horse's hoof. At each blow, showers of red-orange sparks arched into the air. Then he plunged the still hot shoe into a half tub of dark, scummy water, and clouds of heavy gray steam billowed upward.

Quickly he pulled his box toward him, lifted Old Jerry's leg onto his knee and tested the fit of the shoe. Acrid, pungent smoke came from the hoof, but as all farm boys know, it did not hurt. If the shoe was right, the smith drove the nails home with hard, sure strokes, and twisted off the ends where they protruded through the hoof. A big rasp smoothed the rough nail ends. It didn't take long, but I would be happy to hang around, listening to the men talk crops and horses, or learning the fine points of the blacksmith's art.

I didn't mind hanging around the livery stable, either, if I got the chance. There was something about a small-town livery stable that set it apart. In days when drummers came by train with bulky boxes of samples and hired a team to travel to surrounding villages, a livery stable was a part of the town's socioeconomic order.

The big barn behind the hotel was the livery stable in our town. Inside, there was always a pungent smell of leather, hay, and horses. It was good to sit in the calendar-lined office with its potbellied stove and listen to men tell stories. Anyone who kept his ears open could usually gather information to take home. It might be that the pretty schoolteacher was out sleigh riding with that handsome drummer from the city and didn't get in until ten o'clock, or perhaps that Jed Adams had decided to run again for road agent.

The livery man met the train and carried the mail to and from the post office in the general store. He drove the pair of black roaders when the last call came for a resident; he furnished rigs in warm weather for summer boarders who wanted a ride through the countryside.

The old livery stable was more than a commercial institution. Retired farmers made it their headquarters. In stormy weather, farmers came to town and dickered for horses with the owner. It was a forum where free citizens met and exchanged views on politics, conditions of the roads, and whether the new-fangled, snorting, horseless carriages would ever amount to any-thing.

The old livery stables and blacksmith shops are gone. Time marches on and men drive metal machines with portable watering troughs beneath the hoods. But in cities and towns today, there are men who look back and remember the time when a visit to the livery stable was a pleasant part of country living.

January Snow

There are beauties and mysteries in this world which man can only dimly understand. The leanness of a New Hampshire winter landscape, the brooding silence before a winter storm, the awesome vitality of a queen bumblebee beneath a log in below zero temperature—all are integral parts of that period of the year man labels "winter."

Many who condemn snow could agree that a single flake is a thing of beauty. Nature's world is filled with wonders beyond the grasp of man's mind; but few natural phenomena can equal the mystery of snow—a substance created by the solidification of water vapor. In order for snow to fall, the air must be filled with water vapor, the temperature must be below freezing, and there must be a nucleus for each flake. Scientists think this nucleus may be a bit of dust or possibly an electrified molecule.

A snowflake is one of nature's miracles. Billions of flakes fall upon the earth in a storm, but no two flakes are alike. From the water vapor, billions of flakes are formed, and each has a six-sided, basic structure—the same fundamental shape as the bees' honeycomb. Untold thousands of flakes have been photographed and the rule has never been violated: every flake is six-sided but each has variations.

If you have never studied the intricate and beautiful forms of snowflakes, it can be an interesting hobby. Hold a dark board outside a window or door; take it quickly to a cold room and study the flakes beneath a magnifying glass. Each flake is a gem of ordered beauty; each is different from the others. And in their white beauty a man can glimpse a bit of the order behind the natural forces that govern life on our planet.

Snow Rolling

Do you remember when big, bulky, snow rollers went groaning and creaking along village streets and country roads? Half a century ago snow was rolled down intead of shoved aside. If we had a winter of deep snow, come April the snow was still packed on the roads when the fields were bare.

In those days we boys wanted snow for two reasons. First, it meant a day or two out of school; second, we could earn a dollar or two working with the roller. It was exciting after a real storm to get up early, do the chores, and then take the work team up the road to Mr. Adams. He had charge of the roads in our section of town. After a foot of snow had fallen he would use six horses to pull the big double-barreled roller.

Research does not tell when or where the first snow roller was put into use. The earliest reference I have found was to the big hogsheads of tobacco that were brought down from the north country through Crawford Notch in the White Mountains. This was mentioned in Poole's *Great White Hills of New Hampshire*. Apparently tobacco was raised north of the mountains. It was packed in huge hogsheads and then pulled down to Portland by oxen. I gather that the first road through the Notch was made about 1780. It seems logical to assume that when farmers saw how these huge hogsheads rolled down the snow, they built the big snow rollers that we knew fifty years ago.

I remember snow rollers of different sizes. There were small ones with barrels only four or five feet in diameter. There were gigantic ones, perhaps seven or eight feet in diameter. Four teams were often used to pull these. Usually there was a platform on top where the driver sat. On the small roller, the seat was often at the front of the roller, just behind the pole for the first pair of horses.

On a sunny day after a storm, it was pleasant to roll down

the snow. The world was white; the mountains were sparkling. We had to shovel through deep drifts, for along each section of country road there were well-known spots where the snow drifted deep if a wind accompanied the storm.

In the days of good neighborliness, Mr. Adams always swung into the farmyards and made a circle if it would help the farmer. The womenfolk came out with hot coffee and doughnuts or perhaps a piece of cake. There was friendliness in the air in those days before life became so impersonal.

I can still hear the dry creakings, groanings, and squeakings of the big roller. I remember the fun we had during a brisk winter day, and how once in a while Mr. Adams would let us try handling the reins. Today I hear the big, powerful trucks go scraping by. They clear the roads quickly and well, and folks can get to their favorite ski place for winter fun. But I wish that once more I could look from my study window and see six big horses pulling a snow roller along our village street.

Working in the Woods

I used to look forward to Saturdays during the winter. It was not that I did not like school. But unless the weatherman was in a bad mood, those were the days when Father and I took our axes and crosscut saw and went into the woodland.

When I was a boy, we got up early all the time. Five o'clock was the regular hour so the milk would be ready for the man who collected the eight-quart jugs with wooden stoppers. He came along the valley road with his two-horse team in time to get the milk to the depot for the morning train to Boston.

But on a winter's Saturday when the weather was good, Father called me at about four thirty. After breakfast and chores were finished, we started for the woodlot and a day among the trees.

Father was interested in conservation and talked to me as we chose trees to be cut or while we rested. I learned about forests in Germany and how they treated trees as a crop. "Over there," he said, "it is a rule that each time a tree is cut, another shall be planted. Some day forestry will be an important profession in this nation."

I was probably about twelve years old when I first began doing a day's work in the woods, and I remember the stories that Father told which stirred my imagination and led to a lifelong study of trees and forestry. He told me of the vast stands of virgin trees and how pioneers cut and burned billions of board feet. "Cleared land was more important than trees," he said, "and all over the country, east of the Mississippi, great burnings took place."

And he told me how Mother Nature was taking back her own in the northeast. I had seen it myself. I knew of old roads over hills and mountain shoulders where hill farms had once thrived. Now you could see the gaping, granite-wall cellar holes of former homes and big barns. "Most of our land around here is meant to grow trees," Father said. "But we don't think of the future."

Just a quarter mile or so from where we worked was a good example of man's ruthlessness. A lumberman had bought the stand from a farmer. He moved in with his mill and slashed down everything to perhaps four inches in diameter. He left no tall trees for seed trees. He left the brush scattered everywhere, and a year later a bad fire swept the area and killed all the small trees. It was a scene of desolation.

I learned what is meant by "ripe" trees, trees that had reached their full growth and were ready for harvest. I learned about thinning out small trees when they grew too thickly so that a few of the best would have the chance to develop into good lumber.

We used axes and the crosscut saw. I have always liked to use an ax and I was proud of my light-weight Niagara Boy's model. It weighed three and a half pounds. Father's ax was a Michigan Pattern with a curving poll and weighed five pounds.

We used the axes to cut small-diameter oaks, maples, and beeches for the kitchen stovewood. Men and boys who used axes were very particular about their tools. An ax must fit the person who uses it; it must be just the right weight for his strength; it must have a handle that feels right in the hands. The whole must have a balance that lets one chop easily and efficiently. A good woodsman was proud of his ax and took good care of it.

The ax has a long history. It was one of ancient man's earliest tools, made from chipped stone bound to a handle with leather thongs. Stone axes have been found in the relics of the ancient Swiss Lake dwellers and among the Maoris of New Zealand. The axes brought over by the New England colonists were rough and crude, having heavy straight handles, not much different from the type used by the Romans.

It was probably about 1725 when the chopping ax as we know it was developed. Instead of eight or ten pounds, it was five or six pounds in weight. Men learned that a curved handle was better than a straight one. The poll, or the flat area at the top of the blade, was perfected so the head of the ax could be used to pound objects.

I like to chop the hardwoods and see the chips fly through the air and make a pattern in the snow. As you cut into a tree, a fragrance filled the air. Each species of wood has its own distinctive smell. When we chopped the smaller hardwoods, we cut the trunk into ten-foot lengths and piled them ready to haul down to the house.

On the bigger trees, we used the crosscut saw, both to cut down the tree and to saw the bole into lengths that we could conveniently handle. Crosscut sawing is not the worst job on the farm by any means, but it could get monotonous and tiring to saw through a sizable hardwood. Father always got off one of his jokes. "I don't mind carrying you, Haydn, but please don't drag your feet."

The art of crosscut sawing is to pull and not push. As the person on the side of the tree pulls the saw, you simply hold your end so the saw is level. Then at the completion of that stroke, you pull the saw toward you.

I was always glad when Father sent me to the gray birches along the edge of the woodland to get fuel wood. The grays are the outriders of the forest; they thrive in poor, sandy soil. They give shade and protection while young white pines and hardwoods are starting. Then when the pines, oaks, and maples grow large enough to shade the gray birches, these bushes die. That is the law of nature.

Gray birch is very easy to cut. The wood is soft and

porous, and it decays very quickly if left outdoors. But if you get the gray birch under cover early in spring, it makes a quick, hot fire. Mother wanted a generous supply of gray birch for what she called her "biscuit fire." In the summer, the kitchen stove died down after noon dinner. But at supper time Father wanted hot bread, and Mother made biscuits or muffins with a gray-birch fire.

On the whole, I preferred to work with the evergreens. We cut pines, spruce, and hemlocks for specific purposes. The cross-cut saw with razor-sharp teeth bit easily into the soft wood. It was peaceful and quiet among the evergreens, but on days when a wind was making from the north or west, the branches above made music. It was a haunting, alto-key strain that reminded one of the telephone wires' song along the road to the village.

We sawed down the trees, after making a scarf on the opposite side from where we sawed. The angle of the scarf determined the way the tree would fall. "A good man," Father said, "can fell a tree so that it will go just where he wants it."

We used our axes to trim out the trees, and we piled the larger limbs where we could haul them to the house for kitchen wood. Pine, hemlock, and spruce make hot fires, and the crackles blend with a singing teakettle on a woodburning stove.

Sometimes, on a pleasant Saturday, Father told me to hitch up Old Jerry, and twitch out the lumber logs to the edge of the lot and pile them on a bank. Then when it was time to draw the logs to Johnson's mill over on the Peterborough road, we had a place where we could roll the logs down on two timbers to the two-horse sled.

Old Jerry and I liked the twitching out. I fastened a chain around the end of a log, and then he pulled it to the bank. Sometimes a log was frozen into the snow. Then Old Jerry knew that he had to pull sideways to loosen the log. The big muscles in his flanks rippled and the log came clear with a ripping noise. Old Jerry and I were friends; he knew the job as well as I did.

It was good to work among the trees, but I can't truthfully say that I enjoyed wheeling in wood. In those long-ago days it seemed that my sisters were forever calling, "Haydn, fill the woodbox!"

Woodsheds

Woodsheds are a part of America's history. Pioneer settlers looked to their fuel and water supply first of all; half a century ago good farmers wanted to start the winter with a generous supply of split wood for the kitchen stove, and a big heap of knotty, slow-burning, heat-producing chunks for the tall, nickel-trimmed parlor base-burner.

There is something about an old-fashioned woodshed that many men like. The earth floor is inches deep in a litter of bark and splinters, sawdust, and debris. The solidly packed tiers of wood are comforting assurance during the months of cold and snow. There are rich and pungent smells: the bracing aroma of dried apple, the nostril-tickling smell of red oak, the blandness of maple, and the over-all heady compound generates a fragrance comparable to no other on the farm.

I remember the woodshed we had on the farm when I was a boy. I remember the wood chopping, the sawing machine that came in spring, the splitting, and the many wheelbarrow loads I pushed from the pile in the backyard to the shed. It was my job to remember to fill the woodboxes twice a day. Each year the number of woodsheds decreases; but there are still farms in the northern states where well-filled woodsheds provide a sense of security. Gas, electricity, and oil are wonders of our age; but man is meant to work for his comfort in cold weather; and pushing metal levers or pulling a switch is not arduous labor. Modern fuel is too easily obtained. It just doesn't have the significance of a woodshed that is filled with the fuel a man has harvested by his own labor.

The Mail-Order List

I think it was in the fall of 1908 that Father began paying me five cents a week for doing certain chores. If memory serves, that fall, when I was eight years old, I began milking Buttercup. She was a beautiful Guernsey and an easy milker. I fed the hens

FEBRUARY

WHEN THE COUNTRYMAN TEARS OFF THE FIRST SHEET
of the feed-and-grain-store calendar, he knows he is through the
heart of winter. He has no illusions, however, about February. The
second month often brings the greatest cold and deepest snow. In
the northland there are farmers who still fill old weathered icehouses with big cakes of gray-green ice; men hurry to finish the
winter lumbering before a thaw spoils the sledding. On moonlit
nights, great horned owls send their far-carrying, low-pitched
"whoo-hoo-whoo-whoo" across the fields, and foxes bark from
the ridge above the woodlot.

Once in a decade there is a memorable snowstorm in February; a dry snow falls while the north wind howls. Men call it a
blizzard, and the snow and wind cause death, suffering, and great
expense. Wildlife knows how to hole up for a two- or three-day
storm, but cattle and sheep in the open West are hard put to survive. Piercing cold wind takes the dry snow and plays with it;
great drifts are heaped high against barns, corncribs, and houses;
banks of snow are piled against fences and swirled into deep ravines. When the snow is packed, a saw-edged wind sandpapers it
and shapes lines as clearly etched as if by a sculptor's chisel.

Two or three times a season there are days when a cold,
driving wind and dry snow combine to paint a memorable winter
scene. Winter never rots in the sky, says the old proverb, and a
farmer bundled to his ears and fighting his way to the barn thinks
that it is just as well to get winter over with.

As a gusty, sharp-edged wind sends blasts over the landscape, windrows of snow swirl and pivot, hesitate and plunge forward. White swirls run in uneven lines; they skitter close to the surface; they lift a few yards into the air. Sometimes the swirls rush ahead in even battalion lines; sometimes they are broken into small sections and each platoon executes an individual maneuver.

The swirling snow whisks across the open spaces. Gray day or bright, with dry snow and powerful wind the cold dance goes on. Snow forms sculptured drifts along the roadsides; it piles into heaps against icehouses, barns, and silos. It fills the feed lots and makes good insulation against the north sides of the house and barn.

A snow-swirling day is a part of February. The countryman stands by the kitchen window as dinner is put on the table. The aroma of stuffed pork chops and a mince pie warming in the oven revives his spirits. He will do full justice to the meal. But as he watches the snow swirling across the fields and hillsides, he knows what it means. A snow-swirling day may be pretty to watch, but it means paths and roads drifted full again.

Trust the Ground Hog

I deplore the skepticism that I detect among my peers concerning the woodchuck's ability to foretell weather. Weather is probably the nation's number one subject of conversation, and the great majority of citizens feel confidently competent to predict the future. But the first part of the second month is a difficult time to predict accurately. February can be perverse. There are cold, clear spells, but there are also rains and snows. A thaw may come, and you can almost feel the taut chains of winter relax their hold. Sometimes a tempest howls down from the north, and the wind wails in the chimney and whips branches against the house.

Confronted with this kind of fickle weather, a man might as well leave the predictions to the ground hog. If the ground hog comes out and does not see his shadow, it means that for all practical purposes winter is about over. Of course, we may have a few more storms, but that is to be expected. But the ground hog knows it will soon be time to start looking around for a mate.

On the other hand, if he does see his shadow, he turns sadly but resolutely back to his grass-lined nest below the frost line and curls up for another six weeks' snooze. For the ground hog knows, as should every citizen, that if he sees his shadow it means we are in for it. No sense arguing about it; indecision and worrying are hard on the nervous system. Just trust the ground hog and you will know whether spring is just around the corner. Whichever way it is, there's not much you can do about it anyway.

One Special Day

I often wonder why the February thaw has become so important to the countryman, for there are warm spells in the first month as well as in the second. The psychologists can probably explain it in terms of man's ability or inability to sustain long pressures. The year is a cycle of four major rhythms, but while the weather man conforms to the general pattern, he often varies. Sometimes a man grows impatient waiting for signs of spring, and that is why the February thaw is so welcome. After a spell of zero temperatures and wild winds, one morning on the way to the barn a man stops and sniffs the air. By midmorning he is sure. The breeze is from the south; the red line in the thermometer is up in the forties. Water drips from roofs, and rivulets course down the tracks from the woodlot. At high noon the temperature is in the fifties, and a man chopping wood peels off his sheepskin and sweater.

When a warm spell arrives, you can hear the blue jays' far-carrying bugles as they flash across the pasture. Chickadees know that winter is passing, and a mild thawing day is filled with their sweet two-note spring songs as they poke around the old Astrakhan by the hen house. A lonesome crow in the meadow elm sends a hopeful "caw-caw" across the granular snow.

The hollow, echoing sound of ax blows in the woodlot carries far on a quiet, second-month day. The wail of the chain saw rises and falls as sharp steel bites through trees that may have been growing for a century. A hillside farmer, pruning his Northern Spies, Russets and Sheep Noses, looks down the valley as the train scurries along to the city, and even the raucous bleat of the diesel seems muted and softened in the warm February air.

On mellow, pleasant days, farmers let their cows out for exercise, and the plaintive moos of the cows convey their longing for spring. A dog's bark from the farm across the valley sounds strangely close; the musical notes of the village bell float by overhead. No longer do you hear the high-pitched sounds of sled runners on hard-packed snow, or the music of sleigh bells through a winter landscape. The sounds are different now, as if spring's orchestra was tuning up, getting ready to play.

February Walk

If you walk the winter woods on a pleasant, quiet February day, you can enjoy an adventure in living. Look at the sky and see the gradations of blue from horizon to zenith. Look for the colors in the barks of trees, and study the buds on the boughs. Every nature lover should carry a small hand lens, and as you look through the glass, you will see colors in buds that you never dreamed were there. There are reds and golds, maroons and blues, yellows and ambers, browns and grays and blacks. Once you have spent an hour studying the colors of the bud scales, never again will a bud be merely a shapeless dark blot.

See how the trees' branches grow at definite angles from the boles. Study the massive limbs of maples and oaks and contrast them with the slender branches of beeches; examine the deeply furrowed heavy bark of the maple and then look at the smooth, white patches under the bark of the sycamore.

If there is a thaw and the ground is bare, look down at the dark humus beneath your feet. Dig away the top leaves and put your lens to a handful of humus and study its composition. Look for the humble mosses and lichens and the trailing green vines that have been growing on our earth for millions of years.

We take the lichens for granted—humble, greenish-gray plants that seem never to change through the years. Occasionally we notice the bright scarlet heads of the British Soldier Lichens or the gray, coral-like growth of the Reindeer Lichen. We see the unobtrusive plants on rocks and on decaying logs, on the trunks of living trees and on the weathered boards of old buildings. They seem insignificant compared to the easily understood values we attribute to grasses, flowers, and trees.

Ruskin has praised the humble, wonder-working lichens. He wrote, "Strong in lowliness, they neither blanch in heat nor pine in frost. Slow-fingered, constant-hearted, to them is entrusted the weaving of the dark, eternal tapestries of the hills; to them, slow-pencilled, iris-dyed, the tender framing of their endless imagery. Sharing the stillness of the unimpassioned rock, they share also in its endurance."

It may take a lichen half a century to grow a fraction of an inch in diameter. As you study the interesting growths remember that this humble plant of ancient lineage liberates the chemicals from rocks which seep into the humus, and in time feeds the plants which make ours a flowering world.

A moderate day, whether cloudy or bright, is also a good time to spend a few leisurely hours exploring a winter swamp. There is an appealing "feel" in a swamp that differs from that of the woodland or open meadow. You may see the rounded mound-homes of muskrats. When they are covered with snow they resemble igloos. Tall, coarse-bladed grasses that grow from hummocks thrust their spikes above the snow; wind-torn heads of cattails look like shaggy exclamation points.

One of the interesting times to explore a swamp is following a fresh snowfall. You will see where rabbits have traveled and where a fox trotted by on his daily round. Beneath grass heads are the tiny, dainty tracks of field mice, out at dawn searching for breakfast.

Many swamps have islands of evergreens. There may be spots of higher ground where birches and sumacs grow and the chickadees come around and chant that now February is here, spring cannot be far behind. A swamp is different; it does not appeal to all men, but each part of the environment contributes to the whole.

Along a tree-lined brook, you may come upon a quiet mill-pond drowsing through the icy grip of winter. No one knows how many thousands of millponds were built across the nation in olden days. At a strategic spot, a pond was built to hold water for powering overshot or undershot wheels that revolved the mill shafts. Stones were grooved for grinding grain, in imitation of designs brought from the Old World. As far as research reveals, the first sawmill was built in Berwick, Maine, in 1634.

Even in summer the old millponds are quiet. Stones and logs that made the dam have fallen or rotted away; large trees crowd close to the former water line. Some old ponds are thick with willows and alders and dotted with muskrat houses. And yet they are a reminder of a flavorful era of history. Power from their stored waters ground the grain that pioneers brought to the mill on horseback or on ox sled. Here virgin trees were used to build homes and barns as families settled in the valleys and on hillsides.

Now winter birds hunt food in the trees by the ponds. Pheasants stalk the area for weed seeds, and rabbit tracks make ornamental stiches on fresh-fallen snow. Here where men and boys gathered to watch the old miller grind corn and wheat and to talk over problems of citizenship, all is quiet.

A Boy's Winter Day

I have read that within a generation, the average working day will be three or four hours. It wasn't that way on the farm half a century ago. A fourteen-year-old expected to put in a long day, and as I look back over the years, I don't recall that I or any of my friends thought we had a hard life.

Ordinarily, a day began at five o'clock when Father called me. Father went directly to the barn to start the morning chores. It was my task to start the fire in the kitchen stove so that the kitchen would be reasonably warm when Mother and sisters started breakfast and packed the four lard pails with school lunches.

I learned early that good kindling was a major necessity if one wanted to get a hot fire going quickly. Each fall I brought down loads of dry pine branches from the woodlot. Nothing like resin-filled, dry pine kindling to help the oak, maple, and ash get started.

Morning chores followed a definite routine. The cows and horses and young stock were fed; the tie-up was cleaned and fresh sawdust spread under the cows and in the gutters. We brushed the cows' flanks clean and then did the milking. Milk had to be ready by six-thirty for the team that came along the valley road and carried the eight-quart jugs with those big wooden stoppers to the depot.

Sometimes butchering was done early in January; sometimes if we had a mild winter, we waited until February. If the butchering had not been done, I fed the pigs. We had a small house for the two pigs, just above the horse barn. This small building was about three feet high, four feet wide, and eight feet long. During the fall and winter, I kept it stuffed with oat straw and marsh hay. The pigs burrowed into this in cold weather and kept warm.

Breakfast was at seven-thirty, and we were ready for an honest meal. In those days we hadn't heard of calories, and after our cereal, eggs, fried potatoes, toast and strawberry jam, Father and I always wanted a piece of pie or cake, or a few gingersnaps for dessert.

We left for the walk to school a little after eight. In good weather, my sisters and I enjoyed the mile-and-a-half walk. We liked to listen to the singing wires, and we enjoyed the beauty of the fields, meadows, and hills. I can still hear the crunchy, squashy, dry noises as we walked on the hard-packed snow of the sled tracks.

In bad weather, I hitched Old Jerry to the two-seated pung and we all bundled up against storm or severe cold. I spread old horse blankets on the floor of the pung. We placed heated soapstones at our feet, and we had buffalo robes to tuck around us.

During the day, Old Jerry was stalled at Woodward's Hotel, on the main street of Hancock, and at noon other lads and I went over and gave our horses their noon bait. In those days we had an hour's nooning, and after we fed our team, we returned to school and ate our lunches near the big, wood-burning furnaces in the basement.

School was out at four o'clock, but that did not by any means signify the end of the day's work. As soon as I reached the farm and put up the horse, I changed into overalls and jumper and started the evening chores.

The term "evening chores" covers a surprising number of

activities. As I recall the afternoon schedule, the first thing I did was to climb onto the scaffold and pitch down hay for the cows' evening meal and enough for the first feeding the next morning. Then I climbed down the ladder, and up another ladder to the scaffold where the best hay was stored for the horses. Again, I pitched down enough timothy and clover for the horses' evening feed and enough for the next morning. Then I pushed hay along in front of the mangers and fed both horses and cows.

The horse stalls and the tie-up had to be cleaned. Sawdust was spread in the gutters and under the cows. I used enough oat straw and marsh hay to make a good soft bed under the horses. After the cows and horses had eaten for a while, I turned them out into the barnyard for their evening drink. In very cold weather, Mother heated a couple of kettlefuls of boiling water, which I poured into the trough to take the edge off the icy water.

Milking was routine, but it took time. The milk was strained, put in the cans, and set in the water. Last of all, as I recall our schedule, we fed the grain to the stock.

There was another task that did not appeal to me. In the early part of the winter, I had to operate the turnip slicer. Do you know what I mean by a turnip slicer? It is a diabolical contraption, a table with a hinged slicer. It reminds me of a paper cutter. But slicing a bunch of rutabaga turnips is not like cutting paper.

Rutabagas are big, awkward to handle, juicy, and gooey. But Father and many other general farmers in those days believed that it was good for the cows to have something succulent to balance the dry hay and grain.

I can't recall that it meant anything special to me when Father explained that turnips and rutabagas were different. Even today I don't get enthusiastic over the knowledge that a turnip cell has twenty chromosomes and a rutabaga has thirty-eight. It was mildly interesting to hear Father explain that turnips were an ancient crop grown by the Greeks. It is probably useful information to know that Jacques Cartier brought turnip seed to America in 1541 and that the Indians quickly learned to enjoy the vegetable and to grow it along with corn and beans.

Usually we finished the chores by six o'clock, and I have always been grateful that Father believed in doing almost all .the chores before supper. On many general farms half a century ago, it was the custom to do the feeding and watering before supper, but to wait until after supper to do the milking.

My day as a farm boy was not over with supper. After the meal, while sisters redded up the kitchen, I filled the woodboxes and made sure I had kindling and small split pieces to start the morning fire.

Then came the part of the day that I liked. We did our homework in the soft glow of kerosene lamps. And I had an hour or so for general reading. A farm boy's winter day ended about nine o'clock. Mother and the girls placed the warmed soapstones, bricks, and pieces of hardwood wrapped in flannel in the beds. Perhaps we had a lunch of cookies, apples, and creamy milk.

An eight-hour day? We didn't even dream of it. I worked· in the morning, went to school, and worked when I got home. And looking back to those days on the farm, I think I learned lessons that have stood me in good stead.

Farm Shop

A man's ideas of housekeeping are basically different from those of his wife. And if you need proof, visit any farm shop. I don't put my foot down very often, but when my wife volunteers to clean the shop, I muster my courage and lay down the law. As long as his shop is left alone, a man can find anything he wants when he wants it.

A farm shop is supposed to be a cluttered, dusty place. The workbench is a tangled jungle; the wall shelves are crowded with bottles, jars, paint cans, broken tools, and a thousand-and-one bits of material a man saves against a time of need. Corners are filled with tools, bags of fertilizer, cans of creosote and paint. From spikes in the wall uprights hang old burlap bags, pieces of harness, torn horse blankets, coils of rope, wire, baskets and pails. The floor is deep in litter and debris; windows are gray and grimy, and old cobwebs make gray-black, futuristic patterns against the glass.

When a man gets a fire going in the rusty old stove, and the temperature rises to a comfortable eighty, he can spend happy, leisurely hours while February winds howl around the window. Sometimes he catches up on mending tools; sometimes he sits in the big, battered, wicker chair near the stove and looks over old farm journals, mail-order catalogs and the books he bought at auctions last summer.

A farm shop is a place to work, but it is also a place to relax and enjoy hours of unhurried living. It won't be long until the rush of spring work begins, but meanwhile there are days when a man feels justified in just puttering around at a leisurely pace.

The farm shop is a perfect hideout for the confirmed whittler. I fail to understand why the world continues in such a stew when an informal whittling session by the leaders of opposing ideologies might easily provide a lasting basis for a common understanding. State dinners, stiff-starched protocol, and the cautious conversation that mark the high-level social meetings of the heads of various nations do not contribute to the naturalness that is needed in considering everyday problems. These men ought to sit down together and whittle.

Noah Webster defines the art of whittling tersely: "to pare or cut off chips from the surface of wood with a knife." But he makes no distinction between two main kinds: purposeful whittling and just whittling. On a blustery February day when temperatures are low and a bitter wind is swirling dry snow across desolate fields, it does a man's heart good to relax in his cluttered farm shop and do a little whittling.

A whittler sets his own standards and he sets his own pace. If he has a Puritan streak in him, he'll probably do a little purposeful whittling. There are always rake teeth to be fashioned to replace the teeth broken in last season's haying. And whether you need it or not, it's always good to whittle a new harness peg. But if you're in a completely relaxed mood, you can take a piece of straight-grained pine or basswood and simply whittle for the pleasure of it. Both types of whittling have a place, and a wise man uses each to serve his purpose. It is good to feel the sharp edge of a knife slice through clear-grained wood. A man is always master of the immediate present when he has a sharp knife in his hand and the fragrance of dry wood in his nostrils.

Pleasures of the Parlor

You could hardly miss the parlor stove. It was the biggest thing in the room. A handsome, imposing affair, it was tall, dignified, lavishly nickel-trimmed, and had a shining, isinglass door. It sat on a heavy zinc mat against the inside wall of the living room, and the woodbox beside it was filled with knotty, solid chunks that could not be split for the kitchen stove. Mother was happy when Father said one fall evening, "Mother, we've had a good apple crop this year. Why don't you order that new parlor stove you've been wanting?"

The mail-order catalog pulled no punches in its description. "This Brilliant Base-Burner is a nicely perfected model. All the latest, handsomest and best features of every other heater. Excels all others in the nation in appearance and in amount of nickel-work." There was an artistic, ornamental, spun-brass nickel urn, heavy nickel-plated swing top, nickel-dome head, nickel hearthplate, ash door, rails, and name plate. It had an Akron duplex grate and a teakettle attachment.

Part of our nation's history could be written in terms of parlor stoves. In millions of village and farm homes, boys and girls have sat around parlor stoves on fall and winter evenings doing their homework and dreaming youth's secret dreams of life's adventures. Fathers and mothers, grandfathers and grandmothers have sat in their favorite chairs in the mellow warmth of the big stoves, read farm journals, daily and weekly papers and books, and talked of the future and the past.

We all had our favorite occupations around the parlor stove. My sisters and I usually had homework to do, and Mother, when she wasn't answering our questions, was always busy with a pile of mending. It seemed that almost every shirt sleeve and shirt front, the front and rear of long ones, pajamas, sweaters, jackets, topcoats and overcoats lacked a button or two. But all Mother had to do was to reach in her button box and pull out a near match. She had every type, size, and color in that box. Whenever a member of the family realized that he was about to part company with a button, it was pulled off and put in the box. And every time anything wore out, the button was always salvaged before a garment was cut up for rags. A boy with sharp eyes could recognize a button from a shirt he wore years ago. For the most part, the buttons in Mother's box were just the plain, everyday variety, although she had a few fancy ones left over from one of her Sunday dresses. But even if there was only one of a kind, she never threw it away. You never knew when it might come in handy.

Buttons have had a long and colorful history. The Greeks in 1600 B.C. used buttons in the form of studs fashioned of bone or wood and beautifully decorated with thin gold sheets. According to a press item, buttons as we know them today came into use in the thirteenth century. In the sixteenth century button-makers' guilds were organized in France, and since then buttons have been made of almost every conceivable substance. Our national button industry began in earnest with the British blockade during the War of 1812.

Popcorn in the evening was one of the pleasures of the parlor. Mother saw to it that the gleaming kitchen range had a bed of glowing coals. My sisters used the long-handled popper over the heat and in no time the white, fluffy corn filled the popper. The argument we always had was whether it was better to sugar or butter the corn. Father and I held out for sugared corn. Mother made a syrup of melted sugar which did something salubrious to corn that butter cannot do.

But the trouble was that three sisters and Mother outvoted us. Ours is a form of government in which the majority rules, and a vote of four to two is a definite majority. However, a bowl of hot, flavorful, buttered popcorn is very acceptable—especially if accompanied by a glass of cold, creamy milk and a wedge of chocolate layer cake with plenty of white frosting between the layers and oozing down the sides.

Chances are that Indians popped corn long before white men brought higher civilization to them with guns and strong water. Probably by accident, the Indians learned that corn on a hot rock would explode. Experts say that the red men fashioned special dishes in which to pop the kernels.

Fresh-harvested corn does not pop well because it has too much moisture. That is why so many old maids are left in the popper. Corn pops because the water in the kernel changes to steam. The explosion blows the kernel inside out, but too much moisture hinders rather than helps. Experiments indicate that a moisture content of about thirteen percent produces the fewest old maids.

I didn't know all this when I was a boy. But I did know the names of some of the old-time varieties: Bear Foot, Lemon Pearl, Red Beauty, Nonpareil, Blue Rice, Black Pop, Snow Ball, and Silver Rice. Whatever the variety, a boy who had just finished his homework and who had a bowl of salted and buttered popcorn nearby didn't have too much to complain about, even if it was almost time to go to bed.

On many a winter's evening after I had finished studying geography and was reasonably certain of the spelling of Tallahassee, I would get out the stereoscope and further my education with the colorful slides. Not very exciting in this modern age of television, perhaps, but when life was slower, there was time to savor and enjoy the simpler things.

Twice a year, at mail-order time, Father planned to buy a few more slides. Naturally, Mother and the girls wanted something cultural and artistic: a set of "Pilgrim's Progress," "Summer Trip Through Europe," "Niagara Falls from all Aspects," "Views of Switzerland," and "Views of Boston, the City of Culture." But a boy wanted something else to use in the hand-viewing machine invented by Dr. Oliver Wendell Holmes. He was agreeable to the "Life of Washington," "Alaska and the Klondike," and the "China War." But what he really liked was some good, old-fashioned entertainment. It was difficult to decide among such imagination-stirring titles as "Warm Meals at All Hours," "Wonder if it Was Loaded," "One Stick of Gum for Two," "The Bashful Lover," "Gee, This is a Tight Squeeze," "Mouse on Toast." As usual, we arrived at a happy compromise: a little education along with a little entertainment.

The parlor organ belongs to a quieter, more flavorful era of our history. When a family could afford the magnificent Imperial Grand Organ at $50.95, it was a big event and the realization of a long-cherished ambition. It was handsome, elaborately carved, with a beveled mirror and several fancy little shelves to hold dust-collecting bric-a-brac. There were five octaves and four sets of reeds. A 12-year-old memorized the fascinating names of the sixteen stops: Vox Humana, Viola, Flute, Bourdon, Clarinet, Cornet, Cornet Echo, Principal Forte, Diapason Forte, Treble Coupler, Bass Coupler, Cremona, Melodia, Dulciana, Principal, and Diapason.

On a cold, star-lit February evening, friends and family often gathered round the organ, and Mother played the old, familiar home songs and cherished hymns. Voices were not trained but they were rich and true—and people sang because they loved to. Sopranos and altos, tenors and basses blended in "Annie Laurie," "Old Black Joe," "Flow Gently, Sweet Afton," "Sweet Hour of Prayer," and "When the Roll Is Called Up Yonder." There were lively songs: "There Is a Tavern in the Town," "Solomon Levi," and "The Bulldog on the Bank." And when it grew late, along about nine-thirty, the evening usually concluded with that beloved favorite, "God Be With You Till We Meet Again." And as a boy took his hand-lamp and climbed the stairs to his room under the eaves, all the world seemed safe, friendly and secure.

I regret to say that there's no stove and no organ in my parlor these days. But one thing hasn't changed much over the years —the seed catalog. There is something about a seed catalog that sets a man's imagination working. There are conflicting points of view concerning seed catalogs. One school claims that the paper-covered books are as dangerous as the dime novels of yesteryear; the other holds that the catalogs are good for a man's morale while gray-and-white winter days plod along toward another gardening season.

Of course, if one chooses to be realistic, there are certain things about a seed book that can be questioned. The garden rows are geometrically straight; no stones, twigs, or turf clumps clutter the soil. Artists who paint the garden pictures have never heard of weeds. But on a cold winter evening when the north wind is complaining in the chimney, it is good to sit before the fireplace and study the handsome carrots, magnificent heads of lettuce, big ears of corn, and luscious-looking muskmelons.

Naturally, a man promises himself that this year he will have a garden superior to his neighbor's. He resolves that this season he will not neglect hoeing and weeding when blistering July days arrive. That is what a seed catalog does for a man. His best gardening is done in an easy chair on a winter's evening when there is no pressure generated by the need for thinning carrots or tackling the witch grass that is making a jungle of the asparagus bed. The important thing about seed catalogs is that they foster good dreams—and we need more of them in this world of chilling nightmares.

Saturday Night Bath

One major trouble with the social order is that it is too easy to take a bath. Years ago before running hot and cold water became commonplace on farms, the Saturday night bath was a highlight of the week. Or, more likely in the thinking of a boy, it was a low point.

The history of bathtubs goes far back in man's records. Possibly the Egyptians deserve credit for building the first receptacles in which a person could dunk himself. We know the Greeks and Romans constructed large tubs of white marble. On the farm, circa 1910, a lad used a battered tin tub on a braided rug before the open oven of the wood-burning stove.

The tin tub was the same one Mother used for washing clothes. The bath water was heated in kettles and pans on the stove. A lad learned early that he needed plenty of hot water to keep himself warm, but he also learned that he did not want too great a depth. The braided rug absorbed a good bit of splashing, but there was no point tempting fate.

A boy had a choice of techniques. If he were not too tall, he could sit down in the tub with his knees knocking his chin; or he could kneel in the tub and throw handfuls of water over his back. He could also stand and wash himself with a cloth.

Most boys can wash themselves much more quickly than mothers think possible, but that is typical of the difference between masculine and feminine points of view. It was pleasant to dry yourself with a big, rough towel while Shep, the farm collie, licked your toes. Then a lad climbed into his clean union suit, put on a long flannel night gown and hustled for bed.

Sleigh Riding

By the time I was twelve, Father let me drive the sleigh by myself, and few things in those years of buffalo robes and soap-stone bed-warmers gave me more pleasure than a chance to hitch Belle, the Morgan mare, to the sleigh or to the small pung and go to the village. Riding through a winter landscape is a ride through beauty. It was a mile and a quarter to the village, and the first mile was level along the valley farms. A steep hill led from the valley up to the village with its big, white church and tall steeple, band-stand, and village school around the village common.

If you were brought up on a farm and had a favorite horse, you can understand a bit how Belle and I felt when we started out on a sunshiny, winter day with the fields covered with snow and the mountains in the distance sparkling with white jewels.

Not that I did not like Old Jerry and Old Charlie. They were faithful farm plugs and we were very good friends. My conscience did not bother me a bit when I snitched cookies and doughnuts for them. Old Jerry and Old Charlie were dependable workers, but as road horses they left something to be desired. When they trotted, they went up and down in sort of a bobbing motion. Father used to say, "They travel farther up and down than they do going ahead."

But Belle was a topflight roader. Most farmers in those days kept one horse that was good on the road. Belle was a beautiful Morgan, sleek and chunky, with an arched neck and small head. She was full of life and ginger, and after two or three days in the barn, she loved to get out and go.

"Belle needs some exercise," Father would say on a Satur-day morning when other work wasn't rushing. "Why don't you give her a run this morning and bring back a couple bags of mid-dlings. Don't let her out until she is warmed up and gets used to the cold air in her lungs."

Belle pranced around and tossed her head eagerly as I hitched up. She knew that we were going to have some fun. Belle watched as I climbed in, tucked the buffalo robe around me, and pulled the scarf around my neck. I held her down a bit for the first quarter-mile, and then I let her go. We skimmed along, with the sleigh bells making music, until we reached Sand Hill. Then I made her walk.

Occasionally there were Saturday afternoons when I went to the village with Belle, and that brings to mind the races on Main Street in our little village. As I look back, I wonder how much Father knew about these races. An elderly retired farmer in the village raised a Morgan colt or two each year. Mr. Whitaker and I were good friends, and on these afternoons he would be out exercising one of his mares.

When we met he would smile, raise his arm and say, "Would you like a little brush today, Haydn?" You may be sure that I was in favor. We jogged slowly up the street to the foot of Norway Hill and turned around together by the Historical Society. When we were just even he would yell "Go!"

The Morgans knew what it meant. They stretched out and flew. Men at the two stores on opposite sides of the street came out to see the race. We went by the church and Grange Hall and up toward the depot, swung around and started back. The finish line was between the two stores.

I have often wondered what Father would say. Perhaps he knew all about it. The party telephone line was a communication system that has never been equalled. Perhaps Father knew that cigars and dollar bills changed hands on the outcome. Sometimes Mr. Whitaker won; sometimes Belle and I came in a length or so ahead.

A sleigh ride by myself with Belle responsive to reins and voice was one form of sleigh riding, and I guess I would have to say it was the most enjoyable. But there was another form of sleigh ride that was also fun. We called it a sleigh ride, but we used the work horses and the big two-horse bobsled. A dozen or more young people agreed on an evening to meet at the farm, and this time Old Jerry and Old Charlie were the power.

We put board sides on the sled and covered the bottom with a deep layer of hay or straw. Over this we spread old horse blankets and tattered quilts. There was a board seat at the front for the driver, although half the time the boy who was driving twisted the reins around a stake and let the horses go their own pace.

It was wonderful fun with a dozen boys and girls, all warmly clothed against the weather. On a zeroish moonlit night when the stars were blazing in the heavens, and the fields and hills were like fairyland, voices rang out, and bells on the horses' collars made music. Our goal was Peterborough, eight miles distant, where we would have an oyster stew supper in the local tavern.

It was quieter on the way home, but we still had energy for singing and jokes. There are men and women scattered far today who remember with pleasure those sleigh rides of long ago.

February Moonlight

Once in a decade there may come a blending of essential ingredients in February that produces a spectacular, breath-taking beauty beneath the second-month moon. If you could arrange the succession of events, you would first have a thaw, followed by a sharp zero spell to form a hard crust. The moon would be full or waxing near, and the evening would be calm and cold.

On such a night, there is a sense of peace over quiet fields and meadows, open hillsides, and reed-studded lowland sloughs. Light from the yellow-orange moon is reflected in ten-times-ten-thousand crystal jewels in the frozen granular snow. Colors are soft, rich, and glowing: blues and silvers, maroons and browns, ruby reds and diamond whites. A winter landscape has a maturity that you do not feel in summer. It is mellowed and burnished by the sandpapering of winter winds and cold.

Beauty blesses the land on a clear February night when the moon is near full and sails serenely through a starlit sky. A silvery pewter hue lights the countryside. Houses, barns, and silos are starkly etched; fences and walls bind the fields together in a patchwork quilt. In the valley, the willows along the creek form a gray line of stitching.

On a night when the breeze dies away at sunset and the humidity is low, the stars seem so close that a man thinks he could reach up with a long pole and stir them around. Go to a hillside and stand quietly for a few minutes in the peaceful silence. With the reflection from the snow, it is almost as bright as day.

Once many years ago I watched a rabbit ballet in the bright February moonlight. From a hidden spot among thick hemlocks, I saw rabbits dance, leap, and play in an open glade. One moment the area was empty and silent, brooding in the cold, brittle moonlight; an instant later the place was filled with a dozen or more flashing forms that performed gymnastic stunts almost faster than the eye could follow. The rabbits raced back and forth; they twisted and turned; they leaped high, and there was one comic collision mid-air. Some literal-minded persons insist that animals cannot show emotions comparable to those of man; but when the rabbits are playing in the moonlight, it is as if they were letting off surplus steam in the sheer joy of living.

For several minutes the rabbits dashed and darted, jumped and threw themselves about. They took long, low-flying leaps, interspersed with high jumps that reached four or five feet above the snow. Back and forth they raced in wild grace and abandon. Then, the ballet abruptly ended. In a twinkling, the cottontails disappeared. A small glade among the evergreens and birches again brooded quietly in the peaceful moonlight.

Nature offers an infinite variety of weather, and occasionally in February near the full of the moon, there is a special kind of night when unusually large flakes of soft white snow drop leisurely downward. According to my records, such a night occurs only once in four or five years. All through the gray-sky day you can feel the gradual, unhurried approach of the storm. A beautiful, soft light covers the countryside; fences and trees, silos and gates are peculiarly distinct in the gray-purple light. Hour by hour the grayness deepens; the morning breeze dies away by noon. Clouds remain a silver-gray hue instead of darkening to streaked nimbus.

Day changes quietly to dusk and deepens to night, and the near-full moon pierces the high, thin cloud-layer. Then the big, widely-spaced flakes begin to drift earthward. It is a slow, quiet storm and a night's accumulation may be only two or three inches. A man snaps off the kitchen lights and looks across the yard to the fields beyond. Such a night is rare, and he wants to remember it as long as possible.

MARCH

MARCH IS A METTLESOME YOUNG COLT TURNED OUT TO pasture. It exuberantly flips its heels and tosses its head; it cavorts over the earth and twists and turns unpredictably. There are some days in the month of the Crow Moon when the breeze is soft and gentle from the south. Skies are as blue as a peaceful woodland pond in summer, and shaggy, white clouds wander leisurely across the sky. As the temperature rises, water runs haphazardly down the hillsides and creeps into brown clumps of grass.

Then suddenly, the March mood changes. Dark and ominous clouds billow rapidly above the horizon; the rising wind whips itself into a sullen temper, and tall spirals of old leaves and dust are swirled along country roads and across fall-plowed fields. Cold sleet rattles against farmhouse windows, and early-arriving birds seek shelter in the evergreens. For an hour March displays her cantankerous disposition; then as suddenly as her temper worsened, it changes for the better. The sun comes out, the clouds disappear, and the sweetly plaintive arias of bluebirds come from the old orchard behind the barn.

When the robins and bluebirds arrive, when water trickles down the slopes and the wind makes music in the evergreens, spring is on the way. When speckled alders' catkins begin to lengthen and pussy willows appear, you know it won't be long. Spring in the northland shows on the south side of the woodlot as a band of browned grass widens under the climbing sun. Then you begin to hear the music. It is a symphony of blended notes and sounds. Gusty winds are the string section of the symphony, and crisp notes ripple up and down the scale as breezes swirl across fields and around the house corner.

Don't be discouraged when a fresh fall of snow spreads a white coverlet on the meadows and fields, ridges and hills. That's just nature's way of keeping up the suspense. The gleaming freshness of the countryside matches the mood of the higher-climbing sun. White beauty on the hilltops sparkles like a beacon as winter slips toward spring.

As the mellow March winds bring relaxing warmth and the sap drips rapidly into buckets on craggy sugar maples, the beauty on the hills intensifies. And then one wonderful morning the suspense is over. The temperature rises to the high forties or fifties. The sky is blue from horizon to horizon. As a man putters around the barn and farmyard, he can feel and hear the chains of winter loosen.

Icicles drip and green-gray water trickles down sidehill sled tracks. Clouds of steam billow from weather-beaten saphouses crouching among gaunt maples; a lonesome crow in an elm by the creek tosses far-carrying calls into the soft air. Cows in the barnyard rub against the posts, ridding themselves of winter's thick hair.

Toward the end of the month if a man goes out and stands beneath the stars, he may see dark forms winging overhead and hear the haunting cries of the wild geese on their way to breeding grounds in the far north.

Geranium in the Window

Do you remember the cheerful red geraniums that blossomed in kitchen windows? Remember how Grandmother cherished them, fussed over them, and cut slips to start new plants for friends and neighbors?

There is something reassuring about a red geranium in a window. Like a peony beneath the window or a clump of purple lilacs by the kitchen door, it signifies a home. In times when families trekked over the mountains and flatboated down the rivers, there were cherished flower seeds, plants and shrubs that traveled with heirloom pewter plates and the family Bible.

About 1710 the geranium was brought to England from South Africa. For a century little was heard about it, and then in 1825 Lady Grenville began using them in her summer garden. So far as research reveals, the first mention of the flower in America was in a garden book in 1806.

It has been said that anyone can grow a geranium. Perhaps so. But we know that only loving hands can grow the handsome red geraniums on a kitchen window sill. After a long, snow-bound winter, there is something about a blossoming geranium that fits the time of year. Like the breast of a robin or the bright buds of the crocus, it seems to be a hint of all the color and beauty to come.

Barn Doorway

The angle concerning farm architecture that worries me is the newfangled type of pole barn which does not have an old-fashioned, traditional, barn doorway. From March until October, and occasionally on a mild sunny day in mid-winter, a country-man likes to sit for a spell in the barn doorway after a hearty noon dinner.

It is good to listen to the horses finishing up their feed and the rattle of the cows' stanchions. There's a heady, satisfying fragrance of hay and chaff, leather and old wood, manure and dust, stored machinery under the west scaffold, the cow tie-up and calf pens. The hens scratch in the chaff before the doorway, and the farm collie drowses in the sun beside his master. The two cats sit like sphinxes, motionless and relaxed, and a man wonders to himself if cats think while they sit or merely let time pass.

In Old World countries barns are small. But when men hewed homes from the New World wilderness, they built big barns—barns that matched the grandeur of their dreams. A big barn was an expression of the philosophy that a man could live as a free human being, guiding his own affairs, and accepting responsibility for the results. A man sitting in his barn doorway is king of his domain.

Setting Hen

There has been altogether too much futile hair-splitting as to whether a hen sets or sits. Grammarians are a pleasant group of people by and large, but when a hen develops spring fever and her temperature holds steady at 103, a farmer who is concerned about the future of his broilers, roasters, friers, and fresh eggs takes the feverish biddy and carefully puts her on a clutch of eggs. In my judgment, that makes her a setting hen.

There is an art to preparing a satisfactory environment for a setting hen. In a box of sufficient size, you first mold a layer of fairly heavy garden soil, well banked around the sides so the eggs will naturally stay close together. The hollow of the nest should have a half-inch covering of hay chaff to help maintain the heat, and the nest should be made comfortable with soft, pliable grass. Clover and alfalfa are not good materials because the leaves crumble easily and the stems are wiry and woody.

Of course, a man tests a biddy on a few china eggs for a couple of days to make certain her intentions are honorable. Then it is safe to put thirteen eggs under her and let her begin setting in earnest. Each year fewer farmers set hens; it is easy and comparatively inexpensive to buy baby chicks and brood them under an electric, gas, or coal-burning brooder. But somehow, come March, I like to go through the annual ritual. I watch for the broodies, encourage them, and then set a few.

In the days when hens lived in old-fashioned coops instead of modern apartments with running water, ultra-violet lighting and air conditioning, a farm lad and the biddies waged a constant battle. Enterprising hens "stole" their nests. They chose spots far back under the eaves on the hay scaffolds; they favored dark corners in the machinery shed where a lad barked his shins as he climbed over the harrows, hayrakes, and cultivators. One feathered lady was certain to seek a sanctuary in the center of a tangled mass of thorny blackberry canes; another was certain to fly into the icehouse and hollow out a spot in the sawdust in a dark corner.

Hens do not have particularly high intelligence quotients, but many a biddy has successfully stolen a nest and in due time

generations of farmers for fence posts, sills, and wheel hubs. Slippery elm lozenges are still a popular favorite with many who consider the demulcent quality soothing to the throat. The slippery is a rugged, native American tree, and in March its red-headed buds open into handsome, maroon-colored, curlicued blossoms with striking, purplish-tinged anthers.

From spring until freeze-up time there is constant activity in a tree, although in a large specimen ninety percent of the woody material may be inert matter. Every year, whether a tree is five years or several centuries old, a new layer of wood is added to the bole and the outer-bark layer is forced to expand.

Rough-textured outer bark is caused by the growth of the smooth underbark, and the heavy, outer bark splits and furrows in a definite pattern distinctive to each species. Most deeply furrowed are the barks of the black locust and sassafras; shagbark hickory develops an unusual, curled-end pattern that often resembles gray, weathered shingles on an abandoned farmhouse; red cedar bark develops long, slender shreds that swing in the wind. The sycamore is so inelastic that large flakes drop off and expose spectacular patches of cream-gray underbark. The gray beech is one of the few of the 1,182 species of trees in this country that has the power to expand and still keep its smooth outer covering. Yellow and white birches have graceful curlicued ribbons; an old black birch often has square flakes that remind one of a checker board.

Bark has many shades of coloring—from the eye-arresting, glistening sheen of the white birch to the deep, glowing reds and rich browns of sweet birches. Water, with chemicals from the soil, flows up tubes that are protected by the inner bark; other tubes bring manufactured food from the leaves back down the tree to the outermost cells of widespread rootlets beneath the surface of the soil.

To the man with a perceptive eye and a sensitive heart, a bud is one of nature's profound and heart-stirring miracles. Deep snow and bitter cold may press harsh hands on the winter landscape and snow may crunch squeakily underfoot. But on the branches of trees and shrubs, tightly-wrapped capsules of life wait for time to be fulfilled.

The study of buds is a rewarding hobby. Buds come in many shapes, sizes, and colors. Dogwood has plump, pewter-gray buds while the gray beech has slender, brown-pointed lances; shagbark has a glowing, reddish-brown bud; the swamp maples' are gay, scarlet tridents. Lilacs' buds have chestnut-red hues on graceful scales with cream-colored fringes; the poplar has long, pointed buds with a glossy, deep-brown sheen. White oaks wrap their buds in blunt package-clusters, while the forsythia builds its buds in pairs with shaggy bits of exposed bark for decoration. Most buds are sealed in a package with many overlapping scales; but the willows and sycamores have only one scale. Pussy willows with their blue, black, and red Scotch plaid are especially distinctive. Swamp willows have a deep-yellow color; black willow has a deep-chestnut hue splotched with purple.

Man, impatient for the time of flowering and the harvest which follows, rarely thinks of the dormant life on twigs and bushes in winter. Buds are an elemental force of nature. Man can solve many material problems, but he cannot fathom the mystery of life itself. It's only a bud, the thoughtless may say, but in its humble smallness it is an integral part of the world's wonder and beauty.

March Birds

Each person has his favorite omen of spring. Some put their faith in the ground hog, some believe optimism is a mistake until the equinox and the "line storm" have been passed. But to others, including me, the arrival of the first robin is the surest sign.

The robin may not have the appeal of the introspective bluebird, but he has traits that appeal to me. It makes little difference what the weather may be when he arrives; he is unfailingly optimistic and in good humor. Sugar snows may whiten the mowings, but the robin's hearty song tells us to keep up our courage.

Scientists say that our robin is not a robin at all and has no relationship to Robin Redbreast, famous in English literature. Our robin is the largest member of the thrush family with a tawny, not red, breast. But our forefathers labeled this thrush "Robin Redbreast" and that is what he remains. Originally he was a bird of the deep and primeval forest, but when new land was opened up, the robin adapted itself and began to build its bulky nests in trees near houses. From four to six greenish-blue eggs, dotted with faint brown-purple spots are laid. Frequently a pair raises two and sometimes three broods.

On a windy March evening when you are puttering around the yard, you may hear the deep-toned hoots of the barred owls sound from the woodland. Probably the barred owl is the most common of the owl clan, but it is rarely seen because it moves little in daylight. Toward winter's end, the mating and nesting season, the big, round-headed birds sound their multiple-note, haunting calls for hours on end.

Since man became man, he has feared night-moving forms of life. Over the centuries, legends and superstitions concerning birds that fly silently through the darkness have burgeoned. There are some two hundred kinds of owls in the world and about twenty in the United States. The largest is about thirty inches from beak to tail; the smallest, Whitney's Elf Owl, is approximately the size of an English sparrow. An owl's eyes are fixed in their sockets; therefore an owl must turn its head to see anywhere except straight ahead.

The Hooter is eighteen to twenty inches long with a wing-spread of about four feet. He has black eyes, instead of the yellow eyes of most species, and in March the female is probably incubating her two to four white eggs in a hollow tree.

Sometimes at dusk on a late March day when the snow has disappeared from fields and swamps, you may see a big gray bird flying a few feet above the ground searching for mice. The Hooters consume tremendous numbers of field mice, frogs, and occasionally small birds. Farmers shoot and trap the birds, but on the whole the barred owls are beneficial and help to maintain the balance of nature.

It isn't everyone who enjoys the mournful, unhurried, deep-toned hoots that carry through the darkness. But I like to hear the Hooter as I stop in the farmyard after checking the livestock for the night.

On a quiet day in March when the climbing sun starts water dripping from the roofs, the call of the partridge carries far across fields and hillsides. The king of woodland birds has taken his position on a log or rock, and the loud, reverberating drum-roll sounds from the woodland.

It was in the winter of 1908–09 that I became acquainted with this handsome, regal fellow who reminds me of a miniature Napoleon with his imperial carriage, a thrust-out chest, and a beady eye. Our orchard was bounded on the north and west by woodlands and each morning and late afternoon the birds came from the woods and ate the fruit buds of the Baldwins.

That is why orchardists paid boys to shoot the birds. No one knows how much damage the birds caused, but I remember that men with sizable orchards used to say that partridges, or grouse, to use the correct word, caused hundreds, probably thousands of dollars damage over the years.

The male is a beautiful bird. When the cock walks the forest floor, he acts as if he were the ruler of his domain. On a sunny third-month day when the spring urge is strong, he struts along, stopping from time to time to raise his sharp-pointed head crest. He often pauses and raises the ruff around his neck and spreads his tail with its wide band of black at the ends of the tail feathers. I have often watched him walk, slowly and proudly, lifting his feet unnecessarily high.

The female lays ten to fifteen buff-colored eggs in a nest on the ground. One of nature's most appealing sights is a mother partridge with a brood of tiny, bright-eyed chicks walking in the woods. Many times I have seen the picture and watched the mother put on her act. While the chicks scatter and hide under leaves or in grass, the mother flutters wildly about, making frantic noises, trying to lead the intruder away.

So far as I know, the king takes no responsibility for his family. After the mating season, he goes his way. During the summer he stays in the woodlands and along the edges of fields and meadows. He looks much heavier than he really is. A partridge that weighs more than a pound and a half is unusually large.

We think of partridges drumming only in March and April, but there have been many reports of the king beating the drum on clear, cold, moonlit nights in winter. For many years, ornithologists argued about the way the rolling was done. Now we know that the wings do not beat against the body, but simply beat the air.

I can still hear those drum-rolls from yesteryear. Sometimes it seemed that the kings were challenging each other. A bird sounded off from the north side of the orchard and another answered from the west. Today, more than half a century later, I hear a drum-roll sounding from the woodland above my orchard on the slope behind the old barn. I know the partridges have been eating buds on the Dwarf Malling apple trees. In those long ago years, I may have grabbed a gun and gone to look for them. Today, I smile, perhaps a bit wryly. I'll swap the apples for the drum-roll that means another winter is ending.

Cake Era

If change is indicative of progress, then it is logical to conclude that we have progressed remarkably in the last generation. Those of us sufficiently elderly to recall the 1910 era can really appreciate the monumental changes in the past fifty years. I can remember when horseless carriages first began to appear in small towns and solid citizens were sure that the smelly, snorting things would never amount to much because everyone had horses, and what would become of horses if people bought automobiles

The Golden Age of cakes reached its apex about the same time. In those days women did all the baking for their families. Each woman had a cake for which she was locally famous, and many cherished prize ribbons they won at county and state fairs. At church suppers, Grange dinners and box socials, a man with sharp taste buds knew which cakes he wanted to enjoy after the beans, ham, scalloped potatoes, and rolls were polished off.

Mother usually kept two or three kinds of cake on hand. Father believed it was logical to top off a piece of pie with a piece or two of cake—and this applied to breakfast as well as dinner and supper. The cake plate was a fancy affair, cut glass, rimmed with silver and on a cut glass pedestal. Almost all kinds of cakes are acceptable, but if I were pinned down to an opinion, I would still, after fifty years of objective analysis, give first prize to a three-layer chocolate cake with plenty of soft white frosting between the layers, over the top, and running down the sides.

Working Up the Wood

Working up the wood was an annual late winter or early spring task on the farm. During the winter the wood was cut and piled in the woodlot, and when snow conditions were right, a lad hauled the wood on the one-horse bobsled to the yard behind the house.

Working up the wood meant the sawing and splitting. On a Saturday, the sawyer came with his gasoline engine outfit. I can still hear the whir and whine of the saw. The engine lost power as the circular saw bit into a big stick of hardwood. When the saw finally got through, the engine would pick up momentum again and the chug-chugging would come rapidly and emphatically. The saw went through a pile of wood in no time and left the hunks in a great heap, ready for splitting.

It wasn't a bad task—better than hauling dressing to the fields. I set the chunks on a low chopping-block and split the straight-grained pieces easily. Mother wanted both good-sized and small triangular pieces of hardwood for her baking. And she wanted separate tiers in the woodshed of oak and maple, for she claimed one kind of wood was best for bread and cakes, and another for pies and puddings. Gray birch split very easily. I wheelbarrowed it under cover in the shed and stacked it in a special corner for summer use. I split the oak and maple Mother wanted and tossed them into a pile. They could weather outdoors and be wheeled in later.

Tough, knotty chunks were tossed into a heap for the baseburner. A chunk of maple or oak would keep a fire going through a winter night and insure a bed of glowing coals for a quick start on a zero morning. Of course, on a Saturday a young man had to make reasonably frequent trips to the kitchen to see how the cookies, turnovers, and doughnuts were coming along. Occasionally Father might come around to check my labors and raise an eyebrow at the size of the pile of chunks that I considered too ornery to split.

There are men and boys who still use a bucksaw to work up

wood into lengths for wood-burning stoves. A generation and more ago, a lad of a dozen years could always earn a dollar by bucking wood for a neighbor at a dollar a cord. Mr. Sheldon, the neighbor in question, had a wood-burning furnace, one of the few along our road. So I earned a few dollars cutting the four-foot lengths into two-foot lengths.

If you have not bucked wood, you cannot know the feeling as you put the first piece on the sawhorse, set your left leg on the stick, and start the first stroke with the bucksaw. It's not a very comfortable position. Still, a dollar was a dollar; even in those days a young man battled the high cost of living.

A bucksaw is an ingenious and efficient tool. If the teeth are sharp and if the wood is not too hard and dry, an hour of leisurely work with the saw is excellent exercise. As far as research goes, the inventor of the raker-tooth bucksaw was D. D. Terrill of Bangor, Maine. It should be explained that a saw's teeth cut wood but quickly fill up with sawdust. The raker-tooth is designed to prevent this. It is set at a bit of an angle and "rakes" out the sawdust made by the cutter teeth. A good countryman cherishes his bucksaw as he does his favorite ax or hoe.

A cord of wood is eight feet long, four feet wide and four feet high. It is easy to say it, but it takes a spell to saw each of the four-foot pieces into two-foot lengths. In those days I started early and worked steadily with an occasional visit to Mrs. Sheldon's kitchen for a drink of water, hoping, of course, that I might be offered a little something else to go with it.

I know the question that is in your mind. Why didn't Mr. Sheldon call in the sawyer? I don't know the precise answer. It may be that Leslie Carr was busy with other work, as he usually did his sawing in the spring. Or it may be that Mr. Sheldon just wanted to give me the chance to earn a few dollars.

Woodboxes

Progress seems to be a plus and minus proposition. These days a man steps up to a little metal gadget on the wall, pushes a lever, and heat quickly floods the house. He doesn't understand the complexities of a magic contraption that can start an oil blaze going in the cellar. But that, we are told, is progress. The average man can live in comfort without understanding the gadgets, machines, and supersonic devices that serve him.

There is much on the plus side, but when you depend for winter warmth on oil, you can't hear good maple and oak crackle in a wood-burning kitchen stove while a teakettle sings and chuckles. You cannot sit by a tall, urn-topped, ornately-nickeled parlor heater and watch the changing colors of burning ash, apple, and black cherry through the isinglass door.

There are men who have watched the burgeoning of science who remember the woodboxes of yesteryear. I can still see our two woodboxes. The kitchen box had been painted a sort of pumpkin yellow-orange—a common color half a century ago for kitchen floors. Mother was particular about the wood for baking, and I knew what to bring in from the heaped woodshed. The box was about four feet long, three feet wide, and three feet deep. Each morning before starting the walk to school, I filled the box; each evening one of my chores was to heap it high and to bring in kindling for starting the morning fire.

The box in the living room was about the same length and width, but a full foot higher. The parlor heater used knotty chunks that could not be split for a kitchen stove. The living room woodbox was, on the outside, something of a work of art. My sisters believed in flowers, and they had taken odd pieces of wallpaper and papered the front and two ends of the big box. "Don't hit the paper," was a common admonition to a brother who was anxious to finish his chores.

Filling the woodbox is no longer one of a farm lad's regular chores. No more do mothers check to see that they have the right combination of solid, heat-giving wood for Saturday baking. Men and boys no longer chop and saw wood; no longer are woodsheds heaped with stacked tiers. The countryman thinks of the old proverb: wood that a man chops warms him twice—when he cuts it and when he burns it.

Housecleaning

Psychologists inform us that a man and a woman have different nervous systems, and if you need proof, consider the epidemic of annual spring housecleaning. Just why the fever strikes a woman with such force is a problem that a man had better leave alone. One could understand the situation if the house were dirty, but that is not the case. The house is cleaned once a week, and in March it is just as livable and comfortable as it was in October or January. But come March, a man may as well make up his mind that the annual tornado will hit.

I am not a psychologist and do not pretend to understand the mysterious and complicated stimulus-response mechanisms that induce a woman to spend days cleaning an already clean house. It is as puzzling a situation as the motivation that compels a woman to wash the bedroom curtains when the Tuesday Sewing Club is scheduled to meet in the living room. A middle-aged farmer, ripened by the years and possibly mellowed a trifle from lost battles, knows that his routine will be upset for a few days. Spring housecleaning is a feminine ritual, and the wise man philosophically accepts the inevitable and keeps out of the way.

Apple Trees

No one knew how long the old Garden Royal had been growing in the yard behind the house. It was a huge, gnarled tree with bulging, shaggy limbs. The blue-tinged bark on the massive trunk had known the climbing feet of three generations. Over the years, boys had watched bluebirds nest in the hollow limbs.

It may have been close to a century ago when someone bought a one-year slip from a traveling nursery man and his wife said, "Why don't you plant it in the backyard so that I can watch it from the kitchen window." Perhaps she was a bride, and as her children grew to manhood and womanhood, she watched that single shoot grow into a mature tree.

She and those who came to the farm after her cherished the appealing beauty of the pink-and-white blossoms in May. They watched the apples grow to ripeness and listened to the songs of the bluebirds on soft spring days. And in the fall the spicy, juicy goodness of the red-skinned apples was welcome food for the family.

Now the old apple tree is gone. In the fury of a March tempest, the hollow shell of the trunk gave up the long battle. It lies on the granular snow; the trunk is splintered and the thin, tan streaks of living wood are stark wounds that bleed in the sunlight. It lived a long and useful life, and it will be remembered for the joy it gave as it stood in the backyard of a farm home.

Growing apples these days is a complex process with the increasing numbers of insects and diseases, new chemical combinations for sprays and dusts, and consumers that buy with their eyes and not their taste buds. Gone is the era of Pippins and Porters, Snow Apples and Wolf Rivers, Russets and Greenings. Here and there on scattered farms, you may find a few of the old favorites.

On a sunny March day when blue jays are flying above the sugar grove and partridges are drumming in the woodlot, it is a satisfying job to work unhurriedly in the orchard preparing the old trees for another season. It was probably almost a hundred years ago when these gaunt, craggy old Russets and Greenings were planted. They have known many a spring and winter. Their solid, long-lasting apples have been stored in the earth-floored house cellar, and on winter evenings men have gone down to the pungent-smelling storage space and brought up bowlfuls of fruit to peel, quarter, and pass around.

Pruning is a task for a philosopher as well as for a fruit grower. Dead limbs are cut off, along with the straight up and down suckers that my grandfather used to call water sprouts. Sometimes there is a choice between two vigorous limbs, each laden with fruit buds. It isn't always easy to make a decision, but the countryman knows that two strong branches cannot develop good fruit if they are crowded together.

There are still men who enjoy going out to a small hillside orchard behind the barn for a few hours of pruning. Although pruning is a mechanical task, it requires judgment and unhurried execution. A man needs to pause occasionally when near the top of his ladder and look across fields and valleys to blue-green mountains rising to the horizon. He needs to savor the sun and to feel the soft touch of the south wind.

Picking-Over Time

Picking-over time was a recognized part of the farm calendar, and each autumn the farmhouse cellar was well filled with food. Shelves and closets were a colorful display of vegetables, fruits, pickles, preserves, and jellies. There was a big bin of potatoes, a smaller bin of cabbages, heaps of carrots, beets, and turnips. The big barrel of salt pork sat under the cellar stairs and a barrel of vinegar rested on a wooden frame.

However, picking-over time in March was concerned with apples. Each fall barrels of Baldwins, Russets, and Northern Spies were put in the cellar for the winter's supply of sauce, pies, puddings, and for eating plain. Father liked apples in the evening; but time takes its inevitable toll, and along in the third month rotten spots appeared. To prevent the spread to other apples, the ones with brown soft spots had to be sorted out. The badly rotted fruit went to the pigs, but if an apple was only moderately damaged, it went into apple sauce, apple turnovers, and pies.

It was routine, monotonous work for a boy who would rather be outside. Each barrel was tipped over and each apple inspected individually by the light of a kerosene lantern. A fellow kept plodding along, putting the sound fruit into bushel baskets, until the job was done. Picking over apples was an essential chore, but a young man was always glad when it was finished.

Night Boiling

It is only an old, weather-stained, sagging-roofed saphouse among gaunt, rough-barked, craggy maples. The door hangs at an angle and the woodshed lean-to with its lapped-board roof is silvered with time. Moss and lichens cling on the north side of the house. Each summer phoebes build their nest on an inside rafter plate.

It is maple sugar season again, but no blue-gray smoke spirals from the chimney. No clouds of steam billow from open door and windows. It is quiet and peaceful in the old sugar grove.

(75)

Century-old maples hold bulging, sinewed arms to the warming March sun and chickadees and woodpeckers explore the crevices of the thick, furrowed bark.

Fifty years ago, this maple grove on the upland ridge was a scene of bustling activity. Men and boys tapped trees, hung buckets, and when the weather was favorable carried the sap to a wooden barrel on an ox-sled. Through deep snow, until paths were beaten out, men and animals floundered and struggled.

In this old saphouse, fires were kept burning day and night when the sap ran well. Now the brick arch is crumbling and the rust-scaled evaporator pan is littered with debris. Where once happy voices of children rang in the brisk air of snappy March mornings and the mellow warmth of a third-month noon, all is quiet now save for the spring song of a chickadee or the clarion call of a jay.

There were star-bright nights when friends and neighbors gathered for a sugaring-off party, and thick hot syrup was poured on pans of hard-packed snow. Here around the gray, dilapidated old saphouse, good friends laughed and talked, and enjoyed one of nature's sweetest gifts.

Today maple sugaring is an exact scientific process. There are plastic bags instead of wooden or metal pails; a portable gasoline engine bores the holes for the spouts. Sugar makers time the boiling of the sap carefully and use special thermometers to guarantee a topflight product to pour over a man's buckwheat cakes for breakfast.

Time was when a boy looked forward to sugaring season. In a rush period, I was allowed to stay home from District School a day or two to help with the night boiling. When enough sap had collected, Father would say at supper, "Mother, I guess Son and I will have to boil tonight." It meant work, for it was my job to keep the fire going beneath the long evaporator, but I managed to snooze from time to time during the night on a pile of hemlock boughs.

A night boiling was frequently the occasion for a sugaring-off party. Neighbors from up and down the road gathered for the party, while Mother boiled down a kettle of syrup on an old rusty stove. We poured the hot, heavy syrup over packed snow, or boiled it down to light-colored sugar and ate it with raised doughnuts. In between bouts of sweetness you could restore your taste buds with a mouth-puckering dill pickle.

Night boiling was more than just a party and a good time. I remember the darkness in the sugar grove, the clouds of steam, the fragrance of sap changing to sweetness, and the heat of the crackling fire. Today, oil-fired furnaces do much of the work in the big operations, and pipe lines bring the sap to a central collecting point. But there are still farms where men and boys do it the old-fashioned way, and store up memories of night boiling as vivid as my own.

APRIL

THERE ARE WIDELY DIVERGENT OPINIONS CONCERNING THE month of April. Some speak of the fourth month in harshly critical terms; they emphasize the cold winds and pelting rains, spring's timid advances and abrupt withdrawals. I admit that April can be almost as perverse as March, and some years it is a wearisome time from the end of March to the fulfillment of May.

But the day spring comes is a memorable one. The sun is golden in a blue sky; the breeze is gentle and from the south. Crows call from the pasture elms and a hawk circles above. Woodchucks poke slowly about in the clover patch, and pheasants stalk regally along the woods edge. There is a good fragrance from the moist earth. The monotone song of the tractor is heard as farmers plow light-soil fields. A man gets down on his knees to look at the red tips of peonies and rhubarb knobs poking through the dark soil.

Song sparrows call cheerfully from fence posts, and woodpeckers drum on weathered telephone poles. When a man takes ax, hammer, and nails and walks his pasture boundary to mend the fence, he sees catkins dangling from the birches and alders. At wood's edge the skunk cabbage's red-and-purple spathes are lush with maturity; wake robins and trilliums are pushing through brown, winter-sodden leaves.

Pasture brooks run full. They come tumbling and leaping from the highlands and then hurry through meadow lowlands. A man should know a brook in all seasons of the year, but there is something exhilarating about an April brook. In a rocky ravine where the water falls over ledges and drops sparkle in the bright sun, you can feel the urgency of spring.

Brooks are often born on the uplands where springs bubble from a ledge fissure; a small trickle flows from its birthplace and starts downward among grasses and ferns. It flows through upland woods and across open pastures. Other springs join in and the trickles become a brook. Its song grows in volume as the waters drop down toward the valley. Green mosses line rocky banks; maples and oaks guard the sides above. In a succession of small waterfalls, the brook splashes through a cool ravine, half in shadow from the low-circling April sun. In shallow pools, small tan and cream-colored stones move restlessly in the surging water; sheets of gray-green flow smoothly over worn rock. There is beauty in an April stream, and in the music of the water you can hear the quickening tempo of the season.

From now until June solstice, life forces surge forward with irresistible power. Each day you can see the changes. There is soft color as buds open, misty loveliness tints the woodlands as leaves push their way out and change hardwood ridges from gray-brown to fresh, light green. Spring is only one part of the annual cycle, a natural phenomenon. But it is always much more than that to a man who has been looking forward to the time of growth and gardening and green on the meadows.

Spring Tonic

I understand that sulfur-and-molasses has joined bootjacks and buffalo robes on the heap of humanity's outmoded accoutrements. Boys and girls no longer wear bags of powerful-smelling asafetida beneath their union suits. The era of bottled spring tonics is over, too, but a middle-aged, one-horse farmer occasionally remembers bygone days when he joined a neighbor in lifting a glass of Wine of Life.

Citizens of the 1900–10 era read the mail-order catalogs carefully, and even the names of some of the spring tonics were enough to stimulate the blood: Peruvian Wine of Cocoa, Beef Iron Wine, Orange Bitters and Blackberry Balsam. Furthermore, the catalog always asked straightforward, unhedged questions. "Are you easily tired? Do you sleep badly? Is your stomach weak? Is your circulation poor? Wine of Life brightens the eye, tones up the nervous system, clears the complexion and restores health. Almost everyone needs a tonic at some time. Keep a supply of Wine of Life on hand. You will find a constant demand for it." A man who was tired of winter and felt his blood required thinning could easily find symptoms in the list that definitely applied to his run-down condition.

Man still searches for tonics. He tries pills, vitamins, minerals and tranquilizers. I am glad that medical men are ready to serve us if needed. But on these days when you can see spring in the air, the best tonic is to get outdoors, feel the sun on your face, and listen to the robins carol that the new season is here.

April Woodland

It is pleasant to walk through a warming woodland when the April sun speckles the faded leaf carpet. The muted brown and yellow, bronze and gray are like an antique, soft-hued oriental rug. Beneath the moist carpet the magic of life is stirring in the black primal humus on which all life depends. Interlocked branches above the cathedral aisles form a woodland sanctuary. Shadows are thin from the overhead branches, but gray-purple lines run from the boles of the maples and oaks, beeches and birches.

The shadbush glows in dense, white bouquets on the hillsides, along country roads and among the birches and alders that circle meadow mowings. It is a humble shrub or small tree. The gray-green, smooth bark has a distinctive hue and the slender twigs are a deep glossy brown. Usually it forms a shrubby group of several stems but occasionally one finds a single-stemmed tree fifteen or twenty feet high. The white flowers have five strap-like petals with pale, lemon-gold stamens and light, sand-brown stigmas on the pistils. The sepals are sharply reflexed. At month's end the shining, elliptical leaves will be fully opened on their inch-long ruddy stems. The reddish-purple core fruits mature in June.

The shadbush acquired its name because it blooms when the

shad run up the rivers to spawn. Its hard, heavy, red-tinged wood has been used for tool handles, canes, and fishing rods. Western explorers and mountain men dried and pressed the fruits for food. But these points are not important. You will remember the beauty of the white blossoms etched against the pale green of starting leaves and the red fruits of the maples. The suddenly opened, fragrant blossoms are a reminder that nature's color pageant is getting under way.

It is good to escape for a time from the clanging confusion of civilization and to walk an abandoned woodland road. You can find old roads in the woods that tell a revealing story. Sometimes they are in lowland woods or along gentle uplands; more often they are back among the hills, away from the strips of macadam and cement that carry man and his products from one area to another.

Farm homes were built on these thin-soiled hillsides a century ago; men plowed these wooded slopes and harvested grain and hay. In open pastures, cows and young stock, colts and steers grazed. Now the forest has repossessed that which men took for a while. The land is no longer plowed; the road no longer echoes with the shouts and laughter of children on the way to District School. Cellar holes are filled with tangled vines; lilacs by worn stone steps are crowded by birches and alders.

No one knows when the first tree was planted. But we do know that for thousands of years man has planted trees in full faith that he and his children and his children's children would live with their beauty. As families trekked westward over the mountains, crossed river valleys and moved onto the plains, wherever a new community came into being men set trees around town squares and along village streets.

Everyone should plant a tree in the spring, even though as you dig a hole in the soil, spread the roots and cover them, you know that it may be half a century or more before the tree reaches full maturity. After it is set and staked, there must be faithful care; a tree must be watered and fed. Man can shape and guide its development. But more importantly, planting a tree is looking to the future and carrying on the traditions of the past.

April Rain

Scientists say that the water supply in the world is constant and that some sixteen cubic miles of rain fall on the earth each day. The trouble is that the distribution is uneven. Perhaps we shall eventually have rain makers that can produce rain in given amounts at any time. But meanwhile we'll have to get along with April rains.

There is no rain just like a cold April wetting. After a few days of sunny, mild weather, when one is led to believe spring has actually arrived, the cumulus clouds disappear; cirrus wisps lace the sky for a few hours and then change to stratus. They in turn consolidate to dark-streaked nimbus and then the storm begins. Rain comes down in sheets for a spell, and then it drizzles for a few hours; soon the weatherman's temper is riled again, and he sends a steady downfall that beats a monotone chant on the roofs. Meadow brooks and creeks rise to banks' edges and begin to overflow; pasture brooks rush headlong down steep hillsides. Barnyards become muddy morasses and the farm road to the black top becomes soft and mushy.

The rain is good for the year's hay crop, good to fill wells, ponds, and springs. But after two or three days of it, a man stands in the barn doorway and begins to wish for clearing skies. The trouble with an April rain, as with many things in our society, is that it is frequently overdone. A century from now, citizens may smile to think we could not control the weather. But until we can, I guess all we can do is to take the weather we get and try to make the best of it.

I could do with a little less mud in April, too. It is assumed that our year is divided into four seasons. But as any countryman who lives on a dirt road will tell you, the annual cycle is divided into five segments. Between winter and true spring, there comes the mud season. Forehanded families make certain of food and grain supplies; for depending on the winter, mud season can last from one to three weeks. A deep-snow winter means a short mud time; a hard, open winter means that frost goes deep, and the mud season lasts longer.

In the days of Model T's, a lad learned to carry strips of chicken wire during the mud season. A six-foot strip pushed under each rear wheel usually gave enough leverage to get going again. But it was discouraging to progress a few yards and then feel that inevitable slowing, the steady sinking to the running boards.

Each dirt road has its well-known mud holes. Sometimes a man can drive around them, along the side of the road. Sometimes an obliging farmer will take down a few rods of fence so his neighbors can use the edge of a field. But an experienced hillside farmer lays in a supply of shorts and middlings, sugar, flour, molasses, and corned beef. He knows the R.F.D. man will get through some way, and he is willing to wait for the mailman's report on mud time in April.

Annual Horse Auction

In 1908 when I was seven and we came to the farm in Hancock, New Hampshire, horses furnished the power for farming. They did the hauling in cities, and some who read this will recall the handsome teams on big delivery wagons, milk carts, and ice wagons. Perhaps you can remember the eager horses that galloped with the fire engines.

In those days horse trading was a vital part of the rural economy, and farmers took great pride in their ability to trade. The accepted rule was to let the buyer beware. If a man could make a deal in his own favor, it was considered the right thing to do. I am not saying that men deliberately set out not to tell the truth; it was more a case of not telling the whole truth.

On a raw, windy April day when the weatherman was offering periods of sunshine alternating with cold pelting rain, two farmers would meet in a comfortable farm shop and proceed to trade. They never went at it directly. Amenities are important in this world, and middle-aged, prosperous farmers were careful to follow the traditional rites. With the fire burning well in the rusty stove and the temperature up to a comfortable seventy-five or eighty, the men proceeded to the business in a roundabout fashion.

After a casual discussion of family affairs, one of the men might push back his chair and say, "How's the hay holding out, Josh? Heard you was a mite short and was thinking you might trade Old Sam. He must be getting pretty old now. Might be a good idea to get a younger horse."

"Oh, nothing wrong with Sam, Adam. Sam's probably ten now, might be a trifle older, but he's still a good horse. One of the best I ever had. Hadn't really thought of trading, but if someone offered one hundred fifty dollars I might think about it."

"Josh, you can't mean that. Got to have your little joke. I'm not seriously interested in trading, but I might be able to use another horse for spring plowing and haying. I'd think seventy-five dollars would be a fair price."

"Guess you aren't serious, Adam. Old Sam is really a part of the family. He's sound, safe, and dependable. The Missus always wants Sam when she's driving to a missionary meeting or to the Ladies' Sewing Circle. How's your family, Adam? Heard your wife had a bad cold.

"Yes, Mother's been feeling poorly but she's on the mend. Say, Josh, how would seventy-five dollars, horse blanket, and a crowbar hit you for Old Sam?"

"No, Adam. Old Sam is too good a horse to talk about him that way. Guess you don't need one very much." That's the way a horse trade went, and eventually Josh and Adam would agree on one hundred dollars plus a blanket, crowbar, and a set of whiffle trees.

The horse auction was different. The man who ran the livery stable brought in a carload or two of horses each season from the Middle West. They were handsome Belgian and Clydesdales. The horses arrived in March but it took three or four weeks for the horses to get acclimated before the auction. Meanwhile, the farmers dropped in to look them over. Long before the advertised auction day, the farmers knew which teams appealed to them. Big posters advertised the sale, and often farmers from neighboring towns came to watch and buy. All the boys, of course, came with their fathers.

It was a matching of wits and ability. The livery man had spent his money for the horses; he was gambling that he had bought them low enough so he could sell at a profit—the higher the better. Singly, and by doubles, the sleek work horses were brought out to the waiting crowd. The burly, big auctioneer was in his element as he cried the sale. The bids always started low, and it is just possible that the livery man had a friend or two in the crowd to get the bids going.

Hour by hour the selling continued. At noon Father and I ate the lunch that Mother had put up in the two-pound lard pails. After the nooning, the auction continued. One by one the farmers got the teams they needed and wanted, or else concluded that the prices this spring were too high for them.

We don't have horse auctions anymore. The days of horse power are gone, along with fringe-topped surreys and sleighs with their jingling bells. A lad doesn't open the barn door in the morning and hear the friendly whinnying of the horses. He doesn't know the fun of training a colt or feeling a Morgan mare's soft nose nuzzling him. The horse auctions served their purpose, and just once more I wish I could hear Alonjo Whittaker cry, "Are you going to let this magnificent pair of Belgians go for two hundred? Two hundred I've got. Will you make it two ten? Two I've got. Two ten I want? Two ten I'm asking. Sold for two hundred dollars to Galusha Applebee and he's got a bargain."

April Tasks

In the *Old Farmer's Almanac*, April 1844, it says, "If you wish to have a good garden, the sooner the ground is prepared the better. Parsnip and onion seed should be sown early. After the onion bed is prepared for sowing, it should be rolled or trodden down pretty hard before the seeds are sown. Many gardeners complain that their gardens are too wet, which if they would put on more manure, that difficulty could be removed."

Come April, there were many seasonal tasks on good Saturdays, and some were not especially enjoyable. If the ground was frozen in the morning, I hauled dressing from the barn cellar to the fields. A dozen cows and some neat stock made quite a pile during the winter, and the manure was spread on the mowings, on the potato patch, and on that strip of light soil where Father raised kidney beans.

Another April task was picking up the brush in the orchard, and Old Jerry and I spent many hours on Saturday and after school getting the orchard clear of the tangled prunings. Father began pruning the 800-tree Baldwin orchard in midwinter.

In case you were not brought up with 800 apple trees, I'll mention that apple prunings are not as easy to handle as, for example, the young willows and alders that we cut along the meadow brook, or the maple and birch sprouts along the walls that lined the fields. These latter are slender and more or less just a single withe; apple tree prunings are irregular, angular, and do not lend themselves to easy packing in a one-horse farm wagon or a hayrack.

Still, they had to be picked up so we could work in the orchard for spraying, harrowing, propping, and picking. Old Jerry and I plugged along at the task. I folded the reins on the hames posts, and he moved along a few feet at command. When I had a wagonload piled as high as I dared, I said "Come along" to Old Jerry, and he followed me to the ravine at the north edge of the orchard where we piled and then burned the prunings.

On a sunny April day when the soil was too wet to haul dressing, the time came for a boy to run the fences, fix up winter damage, repair barways, dig holes for a new fence, if necessary, and make sure all was tight for the new seasons. Research does not reveal when the term "fence-mending" first took on political implications, but it seems logical to assume that a man who was raised on a farm first applied it to his political standing with those who elected him to office. I sometimes feel that political fence-mending could be more aptly described as fence-straddling. A one-horse farmer on a hillside farm, however, enjoys his fence-mending as a regular spring task.

My grandfather declared that April was the time that nature intended a man to run his boundaries. Since ancient days, when nomadic man first learned to plant seeds and harvest crops and to confine his herds, boundaries have been a part of what one hesitatingly calls civilization. Men have built fences of dried clay, bricks, rocks, and logs. They have used hedges and ditches. In this new nation, men have built stone walls, split-rail fences, stump fences, and bunker fences of logs. Now they use wire, woven or in single strands with an electrical shock.

But whatever a fence is made of, it's not much good if it's in poor repair. It was pleasant on a sunny April day to walk the fence lines and make necessary repairs. It was also good to feel the fresh breeze and smell the fragrance of warming soil.

Digging post holes was another matter. Setting posts of cedar or spruce, tamarack, white oak, or ash can be a tiring job. Half a century ago, the mail-order catalog offered the perfect solution to the problem—the Acme Post Hole Digger. "Unexcelled for easy, quick and efficient work. It will bore a three-foot hole in a minute in ordinary soil. Dumping mechanism is simple and effective. The superior advantages of the Acme in utility, speed, and improved results make it the king of posthole diggers. Warranted to work perfectly in any soil, tough sod, hardpan, clay and among small rocks."

Perhaps Paul Bunyan could push down hard enough on the handle to dig a three-foot hole in a minute, but a 12-year-old quickly learned that he was no Paul Bunyan. Father and the hired man tried the new digger and agreed with me; it was more satisfactory to use a long-handled spade.

Still, it was not too bad a task if a boy was not rushed for time. It was slow work when you got down close to two feet, but there were compensations. You could take a minute to inhale the fresh smell of the April air; you could listen to the birds and watch white clouds chasing each other across the blue sky. Even though there was still an edge of coolness to the southwest breeze, it was good to be working outdoors again.

"Something there is that doesn't love a wall, that sends the frozen-ground-swell under it" wrote Robert Frost, and that is why, come spring, farmers mend their walls. Most of the tens of thousands of miles of walls in the northeast were built of rocks. When land was cleared of trees and rocks, the trees were burned, and sometimes the ashes were boiled down to potash. But rocks did not burn or boil down. Fences were needed and so farmers logically used the material at hand.

When I was twelve years old, and spring had worked along toward time for turning the cows out to pasture, I knew what one of my jobs would be on Saturday. After breakfast when Father had finished his second cup of coffee and tamped everything down with a few of Mother's crisp gingersnaps, he would say, "Haydn, why don't you mend the pasture wall today."

The pasture was a long, rectangular strip between the upland field and the big meadow. It wasn't a pasture to delight the heart of a dairyman; it had many acres of scrubby pine and bushes; there were rocky knolls and swampy spots. But here and there were open glades and south sides of knolls with a fair amount of grass. It was the only area for pasture, and we made do by growing oats and vetch to use as green feed in the dry spells when pasture grass was thin and dry.

Mending wall was an enjoyable spring job. Most of it was out of sight of the house and secure from the eyes of watchful sisters. It wasn't hard work, for the stones toppled by frost heaving were the smaller ones on the top layer. In the old days, the common practice was to put large rocks in the bottom layer, middle-sized in the next, and smaller stones on top.

There were winters when only a few stones were toppled; but there were also cold winters with little snow when frost went deep and many stones were heaved off. It was pleasant work on a day when the flickers were shouting and the song sparrows were singing. A boy had time to explore the woodchuck holes and to cruise around the knoll where a red fox usually had a den and young ones. Not many men and boys mend walls these days, but the old walls will remain, lichen-etched lines of stone stitching together the patchwork quilt of the countryside.

Plowing

The first plows were probably heavy sticks dragged or pushed by human strength; then man learned to fasten the rude plow to an animal with leather or bark straps and to tear jagged furrows in the soil. Thousands of years passed, and man moved across Europe and eventually to the New World. From the Atlantic seaboard, over the mountains, across the heartland, over the prairies and to the Pacific, one frontier after another became a settled part of a new nation. Wherever rifle and ax blazed the way, the plow soon took over.

The steel plow was the symbol of a new order; it turned

black bottom land, and powerful sod-busters ripped apart the tough sod of the prairies. Today a controversy seethes among farmers as to the value of traditional plowing; some claim we need new tools to chop humus refuse into the top inches of soil. But many a countryman still uses the one-horse plow. On a spring day when he clucks to his faithful old horse and the sharp point of the plow slides smoothly into the earth, he is part of the year's most meaningful act.

There are many hillside farmers who still do their planting according to the phases of the moon. Scientists agree there is no logic in doing it that way, but some farmers don't like to take any chances. They believe that the time to plant crops which mature above ground is in the waxing phase of the moon, and that crops which grow below the surface should be planted in the waning phase.

Centuries ago, horticultural writers were penning words about moon planting. In 1522, Oviedo wrote about corn planting in Haiti, "Planting is done in the time of the new moon, for just as the moon grows larger, will grow things planted." Opinions seemed to change a few hundred years later, however. The January 1857 *New England Farmer* said, "No delusion is more prevalent, or more deep-rooted, than belief in the moon. Cut your grass, sow your grain, plant your squashes and beans, kill your pork and do a thousand other things which require smiles of the moon! If you wish your colts, calves, pigs and babies to do well, wean them while the moon is waning! To talk of the changes of the moon affecting the weather and controlling vegetation is unworthy the intelligence of the age and should be exploded."

I suppose they are right. But Grandfather claimed he always had better results if he planted by the moon. No one doubts that the moon exerts a powerful influence in certain environmental situations. A lad, a lass and a full moon in the springtime make a natural trio. Dogs sometimes howl mournfully as the moon waxes toward its complete circle; foxes may bark from the ridges at the full of the moon in autumn, and barred owls hoot their eight-note series on bright moonlight nights.

When it comes to planting by lunar phases, I try to be scientific. But a man who particularly enjoys peas, corn, beets and parsnips doesn't like to take chances. So I figure it never hurts to check the *Almanac* to see what the moon is doing when I get ready to plant my seeds.

Sounds of Spring

There comes a pleasant April day when a man goes forth to mend his pasture fences. As he works along in mellow sunshine, he suddenly hears a familiar song. It isn't the cheerful aria of a song sparrow; it doesn't compare with the rollicking carol of a robin. The plaintive, somewhat uncertain and slurring notes could only be the song of the meadowlark. The bird likes to perch in a tree on a knoll, and in the bright sunshine its golden breast with its arresting black band makes an appealing picture. The male is a steady singer through the summer, and even in the fall chooses a high perch and pours forth his thin song.

The nest is on the ground, usually of dead grasses, and it often has a dome that resembles the ovenbird's nest. The meadowlark's back matches the brown grasses, and one may come within a yard or two of a nest before the bird slips away. The male sings to his mate as she incubates four or five brown-speckled eggs. Sometimes he flies high and sings a medley of musical notes, reminding one of a bobolink's song. After they are hatched, the young birds stay in the nest for ten or twelve days, and then wander around in the grasses until they are strong enough to fly. The meadowlark may not have the appeal of the robin or bluebird, but when a man hears the meadowlark's song, he knows that the time of singing birds has come again.

The redwing blackbird makes its nest in the marshland, and its penetrating, three-syllable whistle is a welcome sign of spring. The males arrive in flocks, two or three weeks ahead of the females. They often stay in flocks, wheeling and circling over fields, marshlands, and orchards, as if under the command of a leader. When they rest for a few minutes on cattails, reeds, or a tree near a swampy spot, their whistles carry far in the chill-edged air.

When the females arrive, the males court them with ardor, bowing, spreading black tails, and showing off their bright red epaulets bordered by bands of creamy tan. The nest is a deep, well-woven basket of grasses and reeds, usually built among the rushes and cattails of a swamp. The young redwings, hatched from pale-blue eggs spotted or blotched with brown or blackish-purple, frequently climb from the nest before they are able to fly. Parent birds make a great to-do about their young as they continue to feed them for a period of days. Many young blackbirds are victims of frogs and turtles. Those that survive soon take to the air and add their loud whistles to the symphony of summer sounds.

Many things can be said about crows, and most of them have been said with considerable emphasis. When a man goes out and sees his patch of starting sweet corn torn up for the sprouted kernels, he knows the crows have been there. Sometimes the crows watch from the woodland and almost as soon as the corn is planted, they fly down and dig up the seeds.

Contrary to popular opinion, crows are not black. If you viewed them in bright sunlight the feathers have a steel-blue, almost violet tinge. Crows are big fellows, often twenty inches long with a wing-spread up to thirty inches. Their nests are rough and bulky, holding six or eight bluish-green eggs. Both male and female are attentive parents and feed the young for a considerable period after they seem fully developed.

The chief trouble with crows is that they do considerable damage. They rob songbirds' nests of eggs and young and they wreak havoc in gardens. The second thing that is wrong with them is that they are too smart. Henry Ward Beecher said, "No wonder men dislike crows. If men wore wings and feathers, very few would be clever enough to be crows."

On one of these spring days you may see a big flock gathered together on a meadow or an upland field for a political convention, and a crow convention has remarkable points of similarity with the noisy political gatherings staged by human beings. It is a rough and tumble, raucous, and probably bitter political fight, as the birds of a given area elect a leader for the coming months.

Through the hours you can watch and hear the arguing and bickering. Dozens of birds mill around, cawing persistently at each other as they press the fortunes of some favorite son. There is continual restless movement as aggressive delegates move from group to group on the ground, but off in a tree you may see half a dozen self-controlled fellows who are the bosses.

Along in the afternoon there is a thickening tenseness. The cawing and jawing decreases in volume and you can sense that the final vote is near. Then the leaders come down from the tree and one seems to be the center of attention. Perhaps he is giving his orders; perhaps he is healing the breaks in the party line. In a short time, quietly and purposefully, the crows fly away to a neighboring woodland. The spring convention is over.

I will put up my scarecrow as usual this spring to guard the sweet corn patch. It always affords a convenient lookout for the crow that is on guard while others dig up the seed.

The drumming of the woodpeckers is a much more welcome spring sound than the noisy cawing of the crows. When meadows are greening, hairy and downy woodpeckers begin their kettledrum concerts. There are prosaic individuals who insist that the woodpeckers are only drilling for food. But many competent observers think that spring fever gets into the woodpeckers' systems and they drum from sheer exuberance as well as to call a mate.

On a sunny day when temperatures are soaring and white clouds are wandering along the sky trails, woodpeckers tap out their messages. The males often choose a weather-grayed, splintery telephone pole beside a country road; they like the hard, shiny surface of an old apple tree trunk or limb from which the bark has fallen. The hairy's drumming is louder and a bit slower than the downy's but their riveting messages shred the air as they tap out their welcome to spring.

Horse-Hair Time

If you remember fringe-top surreys, coal-oil lamps, and sulfur and molasses, you recall the horse hairs that decorated coats and hats in the spring of the year. No matter how thoroughly a lad currycombed the Morgan mare, hairs would fly back through the air as Belle whisked the wagon along the dirt road on the way to the village.

The big work horses, Jerry and Charlie, thoroughly enjoyed the currycombing on a Saturday morning when a boy had time for a long session. The bars had V-shaped cuts which combed the hair smoothly. But come April and hair-shedding season, a special comb with wire teeth was more efficient. Big gobs of hair were easily loosened from the skin and a lad stopped frequently to clean the clogged wires with an eight-penny nail. The sharp wire felt good against the horse's skin and the horse pushed sideways to increase the pressure against his side. Wasn't it Mark Twain who said that scratching an itch was one of life's major satisfactions?

Sometimes you borrowed a neighbor's Dakota Horse Clipper, but my father never favored the close shearing that some farmers gave their horses. Hand clippers were used to trim around the ears and fetlocks, and a special wire card was used to comb out the manes and tails.

Horse-hair time was an annual and expected season on the farm half a century ago. Today boys grease and oil powerful tractors as they ready for another farmwork season. But there are those who look back on the flavorful days of yesteryear and wish that boys could know the fun of currycombing friendly horses.

Pie and Biscuits

In the days when spring tonics were used to "brighten the eye, improve circulation, strengthen the stomach and tone up the nervous organism," a man never felt his blood was suitably thinned and the winter humors banished until he had his first rhubard pie.

Rheum rhubarbarum is a natural tranquilizer. It is difficult to pick a favorite among apple, strawberry, raspberry, peach, and rhubarb pies. Each is, or should be, juicy and just sweet enough so that you can appreciate the true flavor of the fruit, and each pie has its rightful place in the culinary schedule. But rhubarb pie has definite tranquilizing qualities at a time of year when a countryman needs a bit of calming down.

This is the rush time of year and a farmer feels the tensions increase as the green comes back to the fields and the cows are impatient for new grass. If a man comes in to dinner and sees a deep, flaky-crusted rhubarb pie cooling on the kitchen table, his nerves relax, his eye brightens, and his circulation improves.

Of course, a man wouldn't turn down an apple pie if it was offered to him, even though this time of year it's generally made of dried apples. I usually prefer my apple pies made of fresh fruit, and I'm not going to stand up in meeting and argue that a dried apple pie is as satisfying as a fresh one. But once in a while I get a hankering for a wedge of old-fashioned, dried-apple pie.

In the past, many housewives peeled, quartered, cored, and sliced two or three bushels of apples for a supply of the dried fruit. Of the some 15,000 named varieties and sub-varieties of apples, none equals the Northern Spy for dried-apple pies. Slices were strung on linen strings, and shriveled through October's sunny days and frosty nights before they were put into brown paper bags and stored in the attic.

There is nothing complicated about an acceptable dried-apple pie. The slices must be soaked in cold water for several hours. Use plenty of sugar and flour on the bottom crust to insure crispness. The pie should be one and seven-sixteenth inches deep. Be generous with the nutmeg and cinnamon, and toss in a handful of raisins. Sprinkle sugar and flour over the apples and put in some lemon juice to bring out the flavor. Just before the top crust goes on, scatter eight or ten bits of sharp cheese the size of a chipping sparrow's egg, along with half a dozen chunks of butter or margarine.

If a pie is not available, a countryman naturally hopes that after his hashed potatoes and bread-and-butter pickles he will have fresh hot biscuits and new maple syrup for dessert. Maple syrup on biscuits is a good dessert any time of year, but there is something especially flavorful about the combination in the fourth month. Perhaps it is because a man tapped the trees and boiled down the sap to golden sweetness. Perhaps it is because he provided the fuel that changed the sweet sap to sweeter syrup. And then again, it may just be the time of year.

There are conditions involved that sophisticated city dwellers cannot be expected to know. The biscuits must be brown-crusted, hot-hearted and fluffy. Four halves, white side up, are soaked with butter and then generously doused with syrup from an old Wedgwood pitcher. Give a man a couple of helpings of this ambrosia and a dessert spoon, and he realizes why he works so hard at spring chores.

Parsnips

Many people have definite likes and dislikes when it comes to food, and one of the most definite dislikes these days is parsnips. But in spite of vociferous opposition, I will continue my crusade for fried parsnips.

Urban dwellers who have purchased parsnips in the fall and have been disappointed have logical reasons for their antipathy. A parsnip needs to spend a long winter frozen in garden soil. Then when April sun warms the soil and the parsnip is dug, it is ready for eating. Months of freezing weather changes the composition of the parsnip so that it is sweet and delicious.

The parsnip is a relative of the carrot, and probably originated in the eastern Mediterranean area. In the days of the Roman Empire, parsnips were thought to have medicinal value. We know they were grown in Germany in the sixteenth century, and were cultivated by early colonists in Virginia and Massachusetts. When General John Sullivan made his foray into western New York in 1779, he found the Iroquois Indians had stored parsnip roots for winter use.

One trouble with this nation in the spring is that more people do not have fried parsnips for supper. A plump white parsnip, boiled just enough to soften it and then fried in slices is better than sulfur and molasses to banish winter humors. The slices should be fried so the outside is golden brown, crisp, and chewy; the interior must be soft and white. The essence of true spring is in those slices, and the least some of my antagonists could do is to try them.

Moving Out the Stove

I miss the tall, nickel-trimmed, parlor stoves. When I was a boy, their cheerful fires provided needed warmth all during the winter months. But there came a day in spring which I didn't especially like. That was the day when Mother said at breakfast, "I guess we'd better move the stove out today." Why it was necessary to move the stove to the room off the summer kitchen was a mystery to me, but my father and I went at it and followed a well-established ritual.

First off, Mother and the sisters spread newspapers on the living room floor in anticipation of trouble. The trouble was not the stove itself. The unpredictable part was taking down the metal stove pipe and carrying the sections to the backyard for cleaning. There was something about a soot-filled pipe that frustrated a man. After a winter's use, the joints were sealed with soot. You gave a joint a tentative tap or two. No results. Stronger and more determined raps. The joint came apart suddenly, and soot flew out on the carpet just beyond the papers.

Moving the stove itself was slow, but not a difficult task. We used peeled, smooth hardwood rollers to inch the stove from the living room through the dining room, kitchen, and summer kitchen to the backroom. As the stove traveled along, the roller at the back was placed in front; three rollers did the trick safely and easily.

Mother and sisters polished the stove and then covered it with old, tattered, patchwork quilts, while Father and I did the dirty work on the pipes in the backyard. Through the summer the stove sat in the corner out of the way, protected by the quilts. I didn't mind moving the stove out; it meant that winter and the chilly part of spring were really over. But I knew that one day in September Mother would say, "Well, I guess we'd better move the stove back in today."

MAY

MAY IS THE MAGIC MONTH. APRIL CAN BE PLEASANT, BUT usually it has wild and windy days, sudden showers, and cold, raw spells. The green world is waiting. Since mid-April we have been watching the new strands woven into earth's carpet. The shuttle tosses back and forth and gradually the resurrection becomes a reality.

Here among the hills and valleys of southern New Hampshire, spring is at least a month later than it is fifty miles south of Boston. Between us and Lyndeboro is a range of low hills, and I can see a week or more difference within the space of ten miles. Often when we have snow left on the ground, Milford and Wilton have bare ground. I have read that spring advances northward at approximately seventeen miles per day. It does not matter. The fact that is important is that spring has finally arrived.

Each dawn the birds' symphony is swelling toward the fortissimo climax. Redwings whistle in the swale and song sparrows toss their clear arias into the sunshine of a blue and gold day. Dominating all of nature's changes in the physical environment is the deepening green. The meadows are lush with a deep-green hue, and the ledged pasture hillsides are clothed in a lighter green. Along peaceful country roads, fiddleheads are unrolling their fronds—a blend of pale green and cinnamon brown.

Have you watched pines and spruces on a sun-drenched spring day when a soft breeze moves the branches? As the branches move and sing, from a distance you can see varying shades of green—sometimes deep, almost black, sometimes a glowing light green, sometimes almost a silvery hue.

There is magic on upland ridges when birches and poplars, maples and beeches begin to unfold their leaves. Unknown to many, the bud capsules, both leaf and blossom are started the previous summer. Inside a waterproof package, the new leaves are packed and twisted, pressed and arranged to sleep through the months of fall and winter.

Actually, the bud capsule is not completely airtight, for a minute quantity of oxygen is required to maintain life. Each shrub and tree has its distinctive bud formation, and if one takes the time to study the buds, he can see interesting colors and shapes during the dormant season.

Now the buds are broken and the new leaves are starting. When the leaves are small they have many soft, colorful shades. I have seen hillsides that reminded me of a misty Corot painting— grays and silvery greens, pewter hues and thin purples. There is one period in a mixed stand of maples and beeches, poplars and gray birches, when for two or three days I can see a painting of pinks and soft reds, rich browns and pale yellows, and hints of purples and blues.

Soon the colors disappear—except for the greens. Perhaps you have noticed on a hardwood hillside after the colors disappear that for a few days as the leaves start toward maturity you can distinguish each species of tree by the different shade of green. Then in a fortnight or so, all the greens blend together and across a brook-traversed valley you cannot tell which are beeches and which are maples.

I like to walk the acres on a May day when the world is green. The tamaracks in the swale are starting their new needles; and on the west-facing slope of the East Forty, the deep green leaves of the wild strawberries contrast with the lighter color of the new grass. From the height of land near the old stone wall that separates the slope from the pine woods, I look down to the village common with its many maple trees. It is a forest of green above the common, and towering over all is the tall white church spire, gleaming in the sun.

The lawns are a deep green around our old colonial home.

The lilacs are green by the kitchen door and in front of the old gray and brown weathered barn. The orchard on the slope behind the barn is opening its leaves, and I can see the first signs of pink-and-white blossoms.

In the meadow, bobwhites and redwinged blackbirds throw exuberant songs to a cloud-patched sky; queen bumblebees hunt nectar for their first brood; early butterflies and insects search for flowers. Along the meadow creek, muskrat tracks are fresh in the soft, moist soil; alders and pussy willows have already begun to shade the spots where trout lurk beneath overhanging branches. Clumps of birches, old beeches and pasture oaks dot the upland. Here, if you are fortunate, you will see the beauty of scarlet tanagers against the green leaves of the birches; here too, you may see a pair of rose-breasted grosbeaks.

Now, in a May woodland, streams run full between their banks. An ovenbird calls, "teacher-teacher-teacher," a mother partridge wanders slowly along with her brood of beady-eyed chicks, and a painted turtle plods phlegmatically on its way.

The Pipes of Pan

Listen! Can you hear the music? Hear the willow whistles piping along country roads as lads tramp to and from the one-room District School? A boy on his way to school can think of any number of reasons to stop along the roadside, and a willow whistle is one of the best reasons. Country boys know that the best whistles are made from willows that grow beside creeks and brooks or along the edges of pasture swamps. There the juices run thicker and faster between the outer bark and the smooth wood.

You need patience and skill to fashion a good whistle. The bark has to be tapped loose and a V-shaped cut made at the correct spot; a shallow, longitudinal cut is fashioned from the V to the whistle end which goes into the mouth. A twelve-year-old has to have several whistles with different sized and shaped cuts so that he can pipe several tones of different pitch. Whistles always came in handy for swapping, too, but if a boy had a special favorite he kept it in his pocket along with his other treasures.

There were other sights and sounds to tempt a boy half a century ago as he tramped along country roads on the way to the District School. On a windy spring day, he had to stop and listen to the song of the wires. Gray, weather-splintered, woodpecker-drilled poles held the gray wires above fences and hedgerows. Attracted by the music, a twelve-year-old with a lunch-bucket in his hand craned his neck and listened in wonder.

It was all a boy could do to get to school on time. He usually had to run the last few hundred yards to get there before the bell stopped ringing. And, once he sat down and caught his breath, there wasn't much to look forward to except lunch time.

About noontime the boys and girls in District No. 9 gathered around the stove or outside under the big elm and opened their lard-pail lunches. The lard pails were packed with substantial cold roast pork sandwiches, a pickle or two, perhaps a jar of applesauce and a big piece of mother's famous black-walnut cake with thick white frosting. Sometimes there was a wedge of apple pie that you held in your hand and ate point first.

Science has devised more efficient containers for lard these days. If children carry lunches, they have special boxes designed for this purpose. When I was a boy no one had ever heard of a thermos bottle, and children drank from a common dipper that hung on a nail above the water pail. No one knew what germs were, so no one worried about them. The only thing we would worry about was how to sit still for another couple of hours until school was out.

A boy wasn't any too anxious to hurry home either. There were always a few chores waiting, so it didn't hurt to linger a little. Where the peaceful, tree-lined road dipped down into a shadowed ravine, a boy might find an old plank bridge to explore. Gray, weather-stained planks were splintered by horses' iron shoes. The rails along the sides of the bridge were covered with lichen, and beneath the bridge a clear-water brook sang quietly.

A boy didn't want to explain how he got his shoes wet, so generally he first took them off. Then in bare feet he edged along the big rocks beneath the bridge. A frog went kerplunk as it plunged into the water; a big water snake went slithering slowly downstream, its head held high above water like the illustration of the sea serpent in the "Book of Wonders." Sometimes a lad would catch a glimpse of the big, handsome, bright-speckled trout that Grandfather claimed was fifty years old. Slender, silvery minnows flashed back and forth in the water. A phoebe usually built its nest against a timber, and long-legged water bugs skated on the water surface.

Birch swinging was another good way to stretch out the walk home. A generation and more ago, a boy went out to fields and hillsides in the spring and hand over hand climbed the slender bole of a white or gray birch. When he was ten, twelve or fifteen feet in the air, he threw his body out sideways, keeping a firm grip on the swaying tree. Then, if all went well, slowly and gracefully the birch bent over and deposited him gently on the earth. The birch quickly righted itself to an erect position. The weight of a twelve-year-old, or the weight of a winter's sleet storm, made no difference.

The humble gray birches are the outriders of the forest. They thrive in poor soil, filling field corners and dotting thin-soiled hillsides. A gray birch rarely grows over twenty feet high and six inches in diameter. Its branches are short and its slender boles offer little resistance to the rigors of the weather or the enthusiasm of small boys. Nowadays I suppose boys dream of traveling millions of miles into space. But when I was a boy we had a breathtaking ride through space swinging from friendly birches.

May Flowers

May is apple-blossom time. Porters, Pippins, Garden Royals, August Sweets and Russets break their buds and shake out white petals; and a countryman going out at dawn with a milk pail on his arm thinks of the fresh applesauce and tangy, juicy pies that will accompany his noon dinner come late August.

When it is apple-blossom time in commercial apple regions, whole hillsides burst into bloom. It is heart stirring to see thousands of trees in bloom—trees carefully pruned, sprayed, and tended. But perhaps it is even more moving to see a few old neglected trees on a shrub-grown hillside behind an abandoned farmhouse. The apple trees have grown slender and tall among the wildlife that is slowly and inevitably closing in around them.

There are bare, dead branches that hold suppliant arms to the sun and stars—weather-silvered arms that are gray ghosts in the winter moonlight.

When May's warmth and rain bless the land, a few pink-and-white blossoms glow like diadems on the top branches; a few small apples grow during the summer and turn to brown, wizened fruits with the cold of November. In winter, partridges bud the trees and pheasants dig for frozen fruits beneath the snow. Chickadees, nuthatches and woodpeckers explore the hollow trunks, limbs, and shaggy bark. The trees patiently stand on a wind-swept hillside, reminders of yesteryear.

When you see a clump of old-fashioned, purple lilacs holding fragrant blossoms to May's blue sky, you are observing a shrub of ancient lineage. Lilacs go far back in history. About 1560, Busbecq brought lilacs from Constantinople to Vienna. Historians think the lilac was grown in China and Persia long before Christ, for there are words in Sanskrit and Hindustani that mean "lilac." The lilac has a soft, pithy stem and, according to Ovid, lilac stems furnished the pipes of Pan.

Possibly the oldest lilacs in America are those at Mount Vernon, although some plant historians think those at the Governor Wentworth Mansion, in Portsmouth, New Hampshire, antedate those at George Washington's home. After its introduction to Europe, the lilac spread rapidly, and history records that Henry VIII had "six lelak trees" in his royal gardens.

The sturdy, everyday shrub is a flower of home. Lilacs are not pretentious; they signify an era when life was simpler and, perhaps, more flavorful. Lilacs by the kitchen door are as symbolic of something fine and enduring as clumps of peonies beneath kitchen windows. There are many new hybrid lilacs today, but the old-fashioned purple blossoms will always find a special place in the heart of Americans.

Each person has his favorite woodland scene, but few flowers are more hauntingly lovely than pink lady's-slippers in a half-shadowy spot in a peaceful woodland. The lady's-slipper is a member of the orchid family. Some thirty species of hardy orchids are known, of which seven grow in the northeastern section of the nation. The name "orchid" refers to the shape of the largest petal; it is sometimes called the "moccasin" flower, or Venus' slipper.

A century ago, old diaries and journals told of extensive areas covered by the pink and showy slippers. Now because of the ruthless and thoughtless tearing of the plants they are limited to the deeper woods and more inaccessible places. If you are fortunate enough to know the location of a patch of lady's-slippers deep in a moist and shadowed woodland, you have found a sanctuary.

These sunny days the blue flags are part of the beauty of the countryside. Sturdy, strong, and erect, they wave greetings to the beauty of May. Around the edges of sloughs and swamps, beside full meadow creeks and singing pasture brooks, wherever soil is moist, this handsome member of the iris family proudly proclaims the new season. The iris family of the world has some 1000 species grouped in about sixty genera. Except for the cold polar regions, the perennial herb is well distributed over our earth.

The larger blue flag is an extrovert among flowers; it holds its head proudly above the grasses and low growing flowers around it. Writers and poets have praised its distinctive traits; Ruskin termed it the "flower of chivalry" because it carries a sword for a leaf and a lily for its heart. Longfellow described it as "A flower born to the purple, to joy and pleasance." Its beauty is part of May loveliness from Newfoundland to Manitoba and south to Arkansas and Florida.

Grasses are humble members of the plant family, but in their small flowerets there is exquisite beauty and form. There are some 4500 grass species and sub-species in the world, and about 1500 are native to North America. Most of us think of grasses as the plants that produce our hay crops, but the grass family also includes cereal grains, maize, bamboo, and sugar cane.

A grass flower has no petals or sepals. Put a flowering spike beneath a hand lens and it looks like a miniature tree with a main stem and tiny branches. A grass floweret opens only once and most often early in the morning. There is nothing spectacular about grass flowers, but as pulsing breezes send waves of green rippling across the hillsides, and the small, unpretentious blossoms open to the sun and air, they add to the beauty of spring in our flowering world.

There was a time in our nation's history when wild greens were important. After long winter months of turnips, carrots, and potatoes, farm families looked forward to dishes of tangy fiddlehead ferns, wild mustard, lambs' quarters, marsh marigold, purslane, milkweed, and dandelion greens.

The common dandelion and its relatives are found all over the world. The name dandelion is of French origin; the deep green leaves with jagged edges slightly resemble the tooth of a lion —hence the French name *dent-de-lion*. Dandelions, however, have been called other names—especially by home owners who do not appreciate the golden blossoms dotting their lawns.

It would not be May to the countryman without the golden flowers in the lawns and around the garden edges. This is a good time to enjoy a few messes of the greens early in the season. Their tangy flavor is a welcome change in salads, but they are even better cooked up.

Naturally there is only one way to fix a mess of greens. After washing, they must be boiled with a chunk of salt pork; the pork should have a few streaks of lean to generate just the right flavor. Furthermore, for best results the greens should be dunked overnight in water to which has been added a tablespoon of salt. Cook the greens for an hour or so with the cut-up pieces of pork. Then about an hour before dinner time, toss in some peeled potatoes. No use cooking this greenery unless you cook your spuds in the liquid. Give a man a big plateful of greens, a couple of potatoes permeated with the liquid, a slice of fried ham, plus a dessert of a quarter of a deep, juicy rhubarb pie and a glass or two of milk, and he will have sufficient strength to carry on until supper.

Building Character

Every man who grew up on a farm can recall the days when he turned the cranks of grindstones, churns, cherry-stoners, turnip-slicers and one-hole corn shellers.

Turning the grindstone was in a special category. Not so frustrating, possibly, as turning the crank of a churn when the butter refused to "come." But the grindstone meant harder work. Father was insistent on sharp edges, and if the cutter bar of the mowing machine had experienced a rough session in a stony field, the blades were dull and nicked. If the scythes used for trimming along the fences, walls, around trees and along the meadow creek were nicked, it meant that Father bore down hard until the nicks were ground out. It took a good deal of muscle power on my part to keep the wheel going.

No one knows the number of farm lads who have turned the cranks of grindstones, and as they did so resolved that some-day they would be merchants, cowboys, railroad men or salesmen —anything so long as they did not have to sit on an old box and turn a heavy stone against a blade of steel. My father used to say, as he watched me strain muscles when a badly nicked scythe was being sharpened, "It's good character building, son." Perhaps, but most farm lads felt they could develop good character without turning a grindstone crank.

There were a number of character-building activities for a young man half a century ago. I am not saying that twelve-and fourteen-year-olds then were unduly keen about laying solid foundations—any more than they are now. But in those days boys had responsibilities that were a part of the whole pattern of life.

Today many major farm crops are nursed all the way through soil preparation, planting, cultivating and harvesting by machinery. A man does much of his farming sitting on a seat and manipulating levers and gadgets. But in the 1910 era, it was not quite so easy, and the work followed a traditional pattern. As soon as the field corn, potatoes and red kidney beans were two or three inches high, the first cultivation was given. On a suitable Satur-day when the soil was reasonably dry, Old Jerry and I cultivated. I tied the reins around the crossbar between the cultivator han-dles and just followed him along.

Then, a little later, after another cultivation or two, Father wanted the crops hoed. That meant getting out the weeds that grew close to the plants. The soil where we raised Green Moun-tain potatoes was good—very few rocks and comparatively few weeds. I didn't mind a little hoeing around the potatoes after school. The upland area, however, where we raised the beans for Saturday suppers and Sunday breakfasts, was light, sandy soil generously filled with rocks. It was the same on the two-acre spot where we raised field corn.

Now don't jump at conclusions and ask why we didn't pick the stones from those areas. We did—or rather I did—each spring after the plowing. Old Jerry pulled the stone boat and I picked the stones; but there were still many left, thrown up by frost-heaved soil each year. Furthermore, even in this sandy, light humus, the weeds sprouted by the uncounted thousands; I suspect the lush crop was due to the fact that we used generous amounts of cow manure.

So on a sunny late May Saturday when I really ought to have been out in the woodlands or climbing the mountain behind the house, I filed the edge of my hoe and went to it. In those days, it was monotonous work. I hoed out all the weeds I could safely get with the hoe, and then I bent over and pulled by hand the weeds that grew close to the plants. I learned early in life that results speak for themselves. When Father came out to inspect the work, and I had missed weeds, the facts were self-evident.

It was always a good day when Father said we could "lay by" the crops. That meant Old Jerry and I could give the final cultivation and hill up along the rows. I put side wings on the cultivator, and high edges of soft soil were laid against the beans, potatoes, and corn.

If you practice the gentle art of hoeing, I am happy to pass along a few tips. First of all, the enjoyment of hoeing depends upon good soil. In soft soil and with few weeds, it is very rewarding to work along slowly, inhaling the fragrance of the earth and watching the lengthening band of brown, freshly-stirred soil. Second, if you think you might enjoy hoeing as physical exercise, or as a character builder, give yourself the right tool. A good countryman is as choice of his hoe as he is of his ax. The dictionary prosaically states that a hoe is a "long-handled implement with a blade set transversely." It does not mention, however, that the blade must be very sharp, and that the handle, while light in weight, must be sufficiently strong so a man can lean upon it reasonably frequently.

There are those, especially on the distaff side, who do not understand a man's philosophy about hoeing. After a spell of stirring the soil, a man needs to lean a bit and look around. I'll admit that I didn't do much leaning when I was a boy, but nowadays I can take my time and refresh my heart and mind as I work the soil of my garden.

Kitchen Marvels

Mother was reluctant to give up hand mixing and kneading. Twice a week she mixed bread after supper on the kitchen table, stirred it down a couple of times, and then left it overnight for the final rising. In the morning after breakfast she molded the loaves and baked them. She agreed, finally, to try what the catalog called the White House Bread Mixer and Kneader. "Kneads the dough so it is smooth and evenly mixed. Kneads any quantity from one to eight loaves. Easy to turn and requires only three minutes instead of thirty. The dasher remains stationary while the whole receptacle revolves. The White House is simple, sanitary and easy to clean. Shipping weight, boxed, 23 pounds. Price, regular $2.50 value for only $1.68."

Grandfather was never quite reconciled to the burgeoning age of mechanical contraptions. A hand bread mixer and a horseless carriage were in the same questionable category so far as he was concerned. But Mother admitted the mixer was a help, and as far as a boy could see, the loaves that came from the oven were just as light-textured and delicious as before. A crusty, thick, end piece of a hot loaf with plenty of butter and molasses was always acceptable eating.

It was in the 1860's, so far as research reveals, that another mechanical marvel was invented. David Goodell, of Antrim, New Hampshire, after watching his mother pare, core and slice apples, went to work and devised the ingenious little machine that has since become world-famous as the White Mountain Apple Parer. David Goodell became Governor of New Hampshire, and there are Granite State citizens today who say that a man who could invent such a helpful device deserved the honor.

When I was a boy on Mountain View Farm, the parer was

attached to the cherry kitchen table. There was a mounted shaft with a two-tined fork at one end on which the apple was secured. The crank at the other end of the shaft turned the apple against a sharp blade. And I was the one who turned the crank. My sisters had the easy job. They took the peeled apples and quartered and cored them. Then we were ready for Mother's famous recipe for mincemeat.

On a Saturday, when a farm lad should have been down in the swamp checking rabbit tracks or up in the woods above the sugar bush checking on the foxes, it was frustrating to stay in the kitchen turning the parer. However, even a boy knows that life is rarely all black or all white. It was much better to help with the paring than to clean out calf pens. And it was certainly better to turn a crank than to peel apples by hand.

Woodland Brook

There are certain things each man can own in his life irrespective of his pocketbook. A man should have a mountain to which he can lift his eyes from time to time. A man needs a peaceful woodland grove and a sunlit meadow. But when May is blessing New England and the urgency of true spring hovers over hills and fields, a man should have a woodland brook.

There are many kinds of brooks in our region of varied terrain. There are small brooks born of springs on the ridges and hills that tumble down pasture slopes, singing as they hurry down to larger brooks. They follow ravines and cuts; they cross tree-lined dirt roads beneath old, weather-grayed plank bridges. There are mountain brooks, wild and turbulent in spring, that pour down the inclines, swirling over rock-filled beds and digging out soil from high banks where spruces and firs, red oaks and beeches shade the rushing spring waters.

Meadow brooks are a third type. They flow through stretches of good soil left by the last glacier that receded from our region some twelve to fifteen thousand years ago. Meadow brooks receive the waters from the small brooks that come down from the uplands on either side. Meadow brooks join forces and make rivers that eventually find their way to the sea. Sometimes meadow brooks are lined with alders and willows; sometimes the banks are grass-lined.

But my favorite in the month of May is a woodland brook. It comes down from the highlands and then flows along a nearly level woodland floor before it slips down again to a meadow or river valley. The brook runs full but without the feeling of flood water. It winds leisurely around big pines, hemlocks, maples and oaks, and where there is space among the trees you can walk in comfort. In sandy, gravelly soil, the stones and pebbles on the stream bottom reflect soft-color glints where shafts of sunlight reach down through the limb-locked branches of the trees. There are rocks along the sides, carpeted with green moss. Sometimes the roots of the trees are clean-washed by the cold, clear water. Here and there you will find pools where small brook trout flash bright colors or minnows shoot away like silver streaks as they seek protection beneath a bank.

In contrast to lowland brooks fringed with alders and willows, the woodland brook is comparatively open. Along the banks, wake robins nod and jack-in-the-pulpits preach their silent sermons. In semi-open places where the sun reaches to the ground, violets lift blue faces and dogwood shrubs hold gleaming, white blossoms.

Sometimes a woodland brook will have a small waterfall where the water tumbles two or three feet to a pool below. Often the pool is circled with fern and the motion of the air causes the green fronds to wave gently. To these small pools in the soft light of dawn, deer come to drink and the birds to bathe. One of my nature memory pictures goes back to a brook that flowed through the woods between our upland field and the meadow. One early morning when I was sitting by a woodland pool, a male rose-breasted grosbeak came to bathe, and that picture of the rich colors, the sun's rays striking the water, and the silvery spray from the waterfall has stayed with me.

A woodland brook costs nothing to own and its dividends are certain.

Fishing

Fishing is an apt illustration of the divergent viewpoints between male and female. A woman judges fishing by the results in the creel. She doesn't understand that when spring works along to a certain height, a man needs to go fishing. The fact that a man needs fifty dollars' worth of equipment and may bring home a dollar's worth of fish is just a burden that a fisherman must carry.

Fishing isn't catching fish. Fishing is getting out of doors so that a man can feel the sun and wind and the rain on his face. It is getting off by oneself on the edge of a meadow creek; it is following a clear-water, singing brook through a quiet woodland; it is sitting in a boat on a peaceful, tree-circled pond.

Fishing is the chance to get away; it is a time to watch the sky and clouds, the red-winged blackbirds, and a woodchuck poking in the clover patch. You can enjoy the music of a singing stream, the serenity and faith-restoring steadfastness of friendly trees, the green of new grass, the blue of violets' faces along the brook edge, and the challenge of a cock pheasant's crow from woodland edge. Fishing gives a man a chance to get caught up with himself and when he comes home, he knows that a day's fishing has done something for him. And of course, there is always the chance he will bring home a big one.

Meadow Music Makers

There is no bird to campare with the bobolink. He is the comic opera lead; he is a happy-go-lucky individualist who wears his black-and-white opera coat with confident nonchalance. In the month of May before family duties subdue his exuberance, his music tumbles forth in gay, fast-tempo arias. On these warming, sunlit days the bobolink makes music from dawn until dusk. The males fly ahead and when the females arrive from the southland, the troubadours stage their concerts. The notes spill like fireworks from their throats; notes tumble over each as if the singer couldn't wait to finish one measure before starting another.

Bobolinks are meadow music makers while spring rushes toward summer. The female lays four to six grayish, brown-streaked eggs in a nest on the ground. As soon as the eggs hatch, the head of the household gives up his wild singing and settles down to bringing grasshoppers, crickets, and other insects to his hungry family.

When a man walks the lowlands these days to see how the hay crop is coming along, he checks his future land harvest and is grateful that the bobolinks offer a concert above the heading grasses.

When you walk the woodlands in May, chances are good that the ovenbird will be calling his shrill, emphatic "teacher-teacher-teacher!" It is a staccato forceful song that in spite of its exuberance in a quiet woodland expresses well the pulsing urgency of the fifth month. From Newfoundland to Alberta and south to Georgia and southern Missouri, the ovenbird is an interesting early summer visitor.

If you sit quietly among mixed hardwoods and evergreens, you are likely to see the bird come walking along, jerking its tail up and down as it walks. Somehow this bird reminds me of a little bantam hen as it walks on the woodland floor, steps along a fallen log, or scratches in the leaves. There is an orange-hued stripe in its crown; its back is a deep olive green; its breast is creamy white with irregular streaks of black.

Only a few know the beautiful melody of the ovenbird's song at deep dusk when the night shadows are closing in the countryside. The bird rises into the air above surrounding trees and while in flight pours forth a melody that blends with the mystery of the night. John Burroughs was perhaps the first ornithologist to describe this evening song; Thoreau called the bird, which he did not identify, a "night warbler."

In wooing his mate, the male dashes and darts about; he poses and struts, flutters his wings, raises and lowers his tail, and takes short circling flights. Often there is a brisk duel with a rival. Then when affairs are settled, the mated pair build an arched nest on the ground. The nest is difficult to find but the eggs are often discovered by snakes, blue jays, and foxes. The teacher bird isn't as spectacular as some; its song doesn't compare with that of the hermit thrush. But one knows it is May when the clear calls sound from the woodland.

The catbird is the musical clown of the bird family. Like all clowns, this fellow has many moods, and you can never tell what his disposition will be at a given moment.

When a man is working along in his garden, stopping from time to time to lean on his hoe, "Shuball," the male, perches on the post at the end of the pea trellis and begins to jeer and mock. You would think that an intelligent fellow, such as he basically is, would feel in tune with the day. But no. He scolds and grumbles; he sneers and laughs. You wonder what has happened to affect his disposition.

Then Shuball has a sudden change of heart. Out comes a musical, sweet-toned and rollicking melody that blends with the golden sunshine and blue sky. It reminds you of the mockingbird's song. The song has no central theme; it pours forth with vigor and warmth. The liquid notes run up and down the scale; then there are interludes of soft whispering melody, followed by fortissimo.

You listen and smile, for you know what will happen soon. Shuball flies into the lilac hedge at the edge of the garden, and out come the scolding notes of a dyspeptic misanthrope. He yowls like a cat and grumbles in a gruff voice; he erupts guttural noises that remind you of a bullfrog's tones. This is the catbird. He is a handsome fellow in his slate-gray outfit with a reddish-chestnut patch beneath the tail coverts. His mate, "Souanna," is less vocal, but she also has a distinct personality. She is a good mother and broods the four or five greenish-blue eggs in her nest in the hedge.

The food of catbirds is largely land and water insects, but when the wild fruits begin to ripen, they help themselves to raspberries and blueberries, cherries and blackberries. A gardener quickly learns that they are partial to ripe strawberries. At feeding stations, they enjoy suet, raisins, peanuts, and bits of bread.

I do not place the catbirds in the same category with bobolinks, chickadees, and bluebirds. Each bird, like each man, must be judged for its own qualities. The catbird doesn't pretend to be something he is not. He makes music when he feels like it and jeers at the world when his disposition is ruffled. The day's mood is never predictable while he is around. And perhaps it is good for a man to know both sweet music and sour notes as he works through his days.

Hedgerows

In May a hedgerow begins to take on its summer shape. The backbone of the hedge is sapling maples, elms, and birches. Along the sides are alders and highbush blueberries, and on the fringe next to the field are goldenrod, mullein, hardhack, oxeye daisies, and grasses.

There are sidehill fields and rolling areas of upland mowing where the hedgerows stand out. A century and more ago, the fields were mowed each year and then trimmed out along the walls. In the 1800's all the mowing was done with scythes, and elderly men who could no longer take their places in the line that mowed across an area took pride in clean mowing along the stone walls.

I have been asked why the bushes, grasses, flowers and young trees grow so luxuriantly along the walls. The reason is that year by year as the vegetation takes hold, the wind brings leaves and twigs which decay and make pure humus. It is a cumulative process. The higher the bushes and trees, the more leaves are caught. Sometimes a farmer plows an area and before the soil is covered with a crop, the wind lifts clouds of good top-soil and whirls them away. But some of the good soil is caught by the hedgerow growth, and this enriches the earth along the walls.

If you have never followed a hedgerow in winter, go out some pleasant, mild day after a snow and follow a hedgerow around a field or up a sidehill pasture. Except for an occasional white pine or hemlock, all is open and easy to read. You may see the tracks of field mice along the edge where they have searched for weed seeds; you may see the clear prints of a red fox as he has walked along, hoping for a breakfast. Pheasants like the hedge-rows, and follow them down the field after they have come from the evergreen woodland where they spend the night. You can see the nests of birds, wind-torn reminders of the summer when the hedgerow was fluttering with life. You may see silver-gray hor-nets' nests and perhaps a mound by the wall that was the home of a woodchuck.

I am letting a hedgerow develop along our east boundary

next to the pine woodland. Some of you may say that this is not good farming, but I say that I raise one of my best crops on this strip of growing maples, weeds, and birches. I don't have to plant seeds; there is no cultivating and no weeding. And the year round there is always a harvest.

My hedgerow is at the top of the East Forty, a sharply sloping sidehill. At the bottom of the slope, there is another hedgerow along the brook that starts by the barn and goes due north the length of the field, and blends into the swale. Along the brook there are pines and elms, maples, alders, and a wild apple tree. I imagine that in 1862, when this was a going farm, the farmer and his boys trimmed along the brook's edges. Probably every bit of grass was needed for the cows and oxen that filled the old barn. From the size of some of the trees in this hedgerow, I know that close trimming was abandoned more than half a century ago. Perhaps the boys went away to the cities, and an elderly farmer could do only so much. Through several decades the trees and brush have filled in on either side of the brook. Now it is an interesting and rewarding place for nature study.

The next time you are traveling along back roads, look at the hedgerows that bound the level fields, climb the slopes and dip into the ravines. In a hedgerow you can see nature's history written on the landscape. A century and more ago, the gray, stone walls were clearly etched on the landscape. Now the edges have been softened by history and the hedgerows.

JUNE

GREEN MEADOWS ARE STARRED WITH DAISIES, AND ON THE upland pastures wild roses hold pink faces to the warmth of the sixth-month sun. When a breeze springs up from the south, grass waves ripple across the green-gold fields. June is the high tide of the turning year, and the meadows, swamps, and woodlands are filled with life. Brief is the concert at dawn as the purple and gray of the night gives way to morning. Bulky, fog feather beds lie briefly over the lowlands and nestle in mountainside hollows, then stir with the increasing heat and disappear into day's brightness. Dew sparkles on cobweb patterns and pearl drops hang on leaf points.

This is the time of *wawe resin*, the Indian's name for Long-Day Beauty. The sun shines from a bowl of deep blue, fringed with fleecy white clouds that cast fleeting shadows on the upland meadow. Bands of glowing color follow the brooks through the lowlands. Blue flags blend with the soft brown heads of young cattails. Painted turtles lay white eggs in the banks of the creeks, and the black-nosed dace nest in the water's shallow edges.

A man should lift his eyes these heartening June days and feast for a time on the blue-green mountains that stand serene and steadfast against the sky. Many of us walk our trail of years with eyes that barely see above the horizontal plane. In the inevitable treadmill of daily routine, we go round and round like squirrels in a cage. We only half observe the path before our feet and too rarely lift our eyes to the hills.

I know that each man responds to the call of a certain environment. Those who grow up along the coast feel the call of the sea. Those who know the beauty of the plains and the mystery of the desert country have something built into their hearts. And those of us in New England who have spent our lives or a part of them among the hills know what I mean when I say that the mountains are a part of our lives.

While it is still dark-hued in the valleys and at the bases of the mountains, the sun's rays strike the peaks of the hills and for minutes there is a constantly changing canvas of soft, rich blues and purples, pinks, and oranges, shades of green, and a strange blend of steel-gray and cream.

From our kitchen, I look across the fields to Crotched Mountain in the north; from my study window I lift my eyes to Skatutakee in the west. To the southwest, Monadnock stands guardian over the southern New Hampshire hills and valleys.

There are different types of mountain masses; groups that radiate from a center with valleys spreading in all directions, and mountain chains that run in one direction with parallel valleys. There are single mountains that rise in noble grandeur from a level land. During hundreds of millions of years, the earth's crust has been heaved and pulled, twisted, piled up, and pulled down. It is difficult to conceive the history of our planet in terms of hundreds of millions of years; but in 1911, a geologist discovered a cache of trilobites, a crab form of life, that was deposited perhaps 350 million years ago in the Rocky Mountains of British Columbia, in an area that is now 6700 feet above sea level.

You and I can find hope and inspiration, assurance and peace of heart without knowing the technicalities. We can enjoy the flowers among the hardwoods at the base of a mountain: the trilliums, lady's-slippers, Canada mayflowers, violets, and partridge berries. We can find peace in the next higher belt, where the air is fragrant and the tall spruces and firs shade the ground and on a quiet evening the hermit thrush sings his haunting requiem to day. Above the spruces is the scrub belt with the wind-whipped birches, scrubby oaks, and twisted pines. And at the top is the bare rock, wind-furrowed, with a few small alpine flowers in protected crevices and corners.

The mountains and hills rise above the valleys, guarding the meadows and swamps, the valley woodlands and upland pastures. Through the seasons, they remain steadfast and calm, a visible reminder of the past and a peaceful reassurance for the future.

Wild Strawberries

The sixth of June might well be proclaimed "National Strawberry Day" for on that day Governor Winthrop arrived at Cape Ann with the Massachusetts Bay Charter and wrote in his diary, "Most of our people went ashore on the land of Cape Ann, and gathered a store of wild strawberries." One can imagine how welcome that fresh fruit tasted after the weary, monotonous weeks crossing the Atlantic.

Strawberries are members of the world-wide family of *Rosaceae* that includes the apple and blackberry as well as that most beautiful of all flowers—the rose. Cultivated strawberries have a well-deserved place, and a man can be proud of his rows of Catskill, Empire, Sparkle and Robinson berries. Big, handsome, juicy berries fill a box quickly, but I believe no cultivated strawberry has been developed which has the tangy, spicy-sweet flavor of the wild berry. On a June day, I take a battered two-quart lard pail and head for the south slope of the pasture knoll. I choose a well-laden patch, where red nuggets gleam in the sunshine, and proceed at a leisurely pace to gather a harvest.

There is more to picking wild strawberries than the material harvest. It is good to sit in the mellow sunshine, good to listen to the song sparrows tossing their carols from fence posts, good to lift your eyes to the blue-green hills against the horizon. And if your thoughts should wander to the strawberry shortcake you are going to have that night, that is good too. A topflight shortcake is made only one way. Open two hot-brown-crusted biscuits and place them in a soup plate. Spread plenty of butter over the biscuits, and then cover halves with a generous pint of completely crushed, juicy strawberries. Let the strawberry juice soak into the biscuits for exactly fifty-five seconds. Then you are ready to eat. That is an honest strawberry shortcake, and one reason why June is the best month of the year.

One Woodland Hour

This is the time of year when a quiet woodland can offer solace and uplift to the human heart. The leaf canopy is deep green, and summer shadows cover the forest floor. Leaves are still fresh and glowing; time and heat have not drained their beauty. Vireos and rose-breasted grosbeaks sing their June music; small rustlings among the dense shrubs tell of woodland lives moving in their habitat. Reach down and feel the surface carpet of dried, faded, brittle leaves. Inhale the aroma of the woodland—a pungent, satisfying fragrance. One woodland hour can be an experience in living.

A woodland floor represents the eternal cycle of life. Perhaps for thousands of years trees have been growing here. A century ago this big oak was a small acorn. After a winter beneath the snow, it struck down a slender white root and lifted a green stem. Over the decades it has grown into a mighty tree. Eventually, unless the tree is cut by man, it will fall to the earth which has given it sustenance. In due time, the tree's cells will change back to humus and the minerals salts will again be incorporated in the humus of the forest floor.

Each year we learn more about the miracles in fungi and bacteria; each year miracle-working antibiotics are developed from fungi. Beneath the brittle leaves that cover black soil, many insects live. There are probably still undiscovered enzymes and hormones that play roles in human life. Ferns and flowers offer their beauty and shrubs blossom in shadowy glades and glens. Here on the woodland floor is the complete cycle: birth, growth, fruition, and return to the soil. It is a cycle of peace and order—nature's plan that man someday will accept, and from it learn to live in peace with his brothers.

When you walk a quiet, shadow-dappled woodland these summer-threshold days, you often see small, slender saplings stretching toward the light. Each season uncounted billions of tree seeds are matured; each year the seeds are carried by wind or gravity to a resting place.

It is one facet of nature's wisdom that seeds are produced in prodigal numbers, for the vast majority do not find a place which engenders new life. Some forms of new life, like the succulent-stemmed saplings in the shadowed environment or woodlands, struggle desperately to capture sufficient sunlight so that the magic of chlorophyll can manufacture food.

Each deciduous tree and shrub species has a typical leaf formation, but in the dim light of the woodland, nature compensates by growing larger leaves. Small saplings grow leaves twice and three times the normal size. Look at a slender, fragile stem of the maple, oak or sycamore. A small, soft green shoot filled with life juices holds a few oversized leaves. Overhead, branches and leaves of mature trees block rays from the life-sustaining sun. The stem or trunk of the starting tree is pulpy and moist. The little trees reaching upward to the sun fight a valiant battle for a few years; then most of them return to enrich the soil that gave them birth.

Some men may think that this is a tragic picture. But as you walk a peaceful woodland you should remember that the picture is part of the integral mystery of life.

Marching Evergreens

You see them on the hillsides, marching down in serried ranks from the heights above. You see them on upland fields, re-possessing land that a few generations ago man took for his use. You see them on lowland areas where men have tried to wrest a living from sandy soil and have surrendered the land again to the trees.

Scientists tell us that millions of years ago a vast evergreen belt circled this planet. Today, they say, we are in the twilight era of the pines and hemlocks, spruces and firs, but as a man watches the evergreens march down a mountain slope he does not worry. In the rear are tall, mature, seed-bearing trees. Each year the imbricated cones open, and seeds float out ahead of the marching ranks. In the middle group are the younger trees, establishing themselves as they take over the pasture areas cleared by farmers years ago. In the front ranks are the small trees—scouts ahead of the main body of troops. Each little tree is a replica of the tall evergreens behind. Nature is infinitely patient, and in due course these small trees will send their seeds forth on a pulsing wind to start new forward ranks.

Down from the heights they march. Year by year they take over the slopes. Across abandoned pastures and mowing fields, the ranks step forward—slowly but steadily. Nature does not like bare land; grasses and trees are the blessing of the earth. The marching evergreens are one more proof of nature's wisdom that proclaims each type of terrain shall grow that which is best adapted to the environment.

Old Swimming Hole

A twelve-year-old's attitude toward water is based on logic. In the late fall and winter it is a senseless waste of time and energy to get wet all over on Saturday nights. A fellow wears a heavy union suit twenty-four hours a day, and very little dirt is going to get through one's outside clothes and underwear. But when brook water warms up a bit, a boy can logically take two or even three baths a day in the meadow swimming pool.

Our pool was a wide place in the creek, formed long ago at a strategic spot. Perhaps water pouring over a rock ledge in spring freshet time had gradually gouged out the brook bed and formed the circular pool. On one side was a big black willow tree with a hollow trunk. Grandfather said he could remember when the huge, spreading tree was a young and slender sapling. Now it shaded the pool in the late afternoon, and even while a lad had his swim, a kingfisher sat patiently on a branch, waiting for a perch to show in the water.

A swimming hole isn't scientifically handled like a modern tiled swimming pool. No one regulates the flow of water or pours in cans of disinfectant. Nature managed the old swimming hole in the meadow, and the water was always cold and bracing, even in hot weather. In spring, snow-melting time, the creek ran full and boisterously; by August, the water ran quietly and slowly between gray banks; but the swimming hole was always full. It may be that the gray-black blood-suckers were a little more numerous, but that was the least of a lad's worries.

Sometimes a muskrat dug a tunnel in the bank, and the rat-tailed little animals swam unhurriedly to their den as a lad appeared on the bank and stripped off overalls and sneakers. There are many strange and paradoxical things about a twelve-year-old. Father used to say, "There's nothing more remarkable than the way a boy can regain his strength when it is time for a swim." It is true. Many a lad who has come to the absolute end of his strength thinning and hoeing turnips, or brushing out along a fence, has revived when his father said, "That's pretty good for today. Better get your swim and bring home the cows." Then a boy raced across the meadow with Shep at his heels. He peeled off his clothes, paused a minute on the bank, and dived into the cold, clear water. After he had splashed around to his heart's content, he pulled his clothes back on and headed for the cows.

The Golden Grains

Nature students are always interested in birds and flowers, trees and insects; but few have studied the golden grains that mean life itself to the billions of plants that form a protective covering on the soil surface. The wonder and glory of the plant life that surrounds us is not always the color of the blossoms, not always the beauty of the flowers, shrubs, grasses, or trees. Important as these things are to our enjoyment, both summer and winter, the true glory of plant life is the functional action. We rarely think of it, but plants, like animals, live according to the laws of eugenics. Plants must reproduce their kind and all the color, beauty, and appeal that we see is secondary to nature's basic law.

In early spring, you have seen the yellow grains on a quiet woodland pond where willows have shed their pollen. You have arranged a bouquet of flowers on a dark mahogany table and seen the golden nuggets against the glistening wood. Perhaps you have stood on a hillside among white pines when their candles of blossoms were lighted, and have seen a gust of wind lift a cloud of the golden grains.

So far as my research goes, the smallest pollen grains are those of the violet, about one-ten-thousandth of an inch in diameter. The largest pollen grains are those of the common pumpkin; if you have sharp eyes you can see them without a magnifying glass. Contrary to what many think, the size of the plant has no relationship to the size of the pollen. The 300–foot sequoia of California has a pollen grain about the same size as the common violet.

If you have never studied pollen beneath a microscope, it is an interesting experience to observe the difference in shapes. Each has its distinctive shape. There are shapes resembling baseballs, football helmets, tri-cornered mince turnovers, waterwings, and spiked marbles. There is even one that resembles a dug-out canoe.

If you are sensitive to the beauty of our flowering world and the cycles of the turning years, you should pause these June days and think of the miracles that are happening all around. For man, with his ever-increasing knowledge of material facts, must stand in reverent wonder before the secret of life itself.

Wooden Watering Troughs

Do you remember the old weather-stained water troughs on the side of a country road, usually below a bushy bank in a woodland? They were made of two-inch, dry white oak or rock maple planks and the water swelled the joints tight. The water came from a never-failing spring on the slope above and the old-timers had fashioned wooden pump logs to carry the water to the trough. The six-inch diameter logs were bored with long-handled iron augers, and one end of each six- or eight-foot log was pointed and fitted into the reamed end of the next section.

The overflow from the trough trickled from a hole near the top and made a muddy section for a way beside the road. In summer, lush growth of interrupted ferns formed a bank of green. In the early spring, skunk cabbages raised their heads above the muddy soil, and sometimes pink lady's-slippers dotted the bank below.

A farm boy on the way to District School always stopped to examine the trough. He pressed his face into the water, held his breath, opened his eyes, and surveyed the underwater scene. Slender green tendrils grew from the sides of the trough and waved slowly back and forth in the water. The sides were thick with a greenish, slimy looking growth. The bottom of the trough was covered with grayish, fine-textured silt that had formed into ridges and gullies. The scene at the bottom resembled those gray topographical maps in the geography books at school.

Naturally, a watering trough was a spot for frogs, minnows and trout. The frogs came and went, but boys watched the fish grow during the summer and took them out in the late fall and returned them to a nearby brook. It was understood that you were not to catch a trout in the trough, and a young fisherman tossed a few angleworms into the trough as he passed by on his way to the trout stream.

Sometimes a boy put a water snake in the trough and then hid in the bushes as a farmer came along with his team. On a hot day, the horses pushed their noses into the cold water and then drew back with a snort. The farmer climbed down, looked into the water and fished out the snake. Perhaps he smiled a bit thinking of the long-ago days when he did the same thing.

It is a different world today. Time has changed the nation's way of living, and horses no longer stop at watering troughs. A car's radiator needs water, but it can't plunge its head into a trough of cold water by the side of the road, and blow and snort in satisfaction when it has had a drink.

Meadow Music

Go into a peaceful meadow and sit for a time among the blossoming grasses. It takes a few minutes for human ears to become attuned to earth's quiet melodies. At first you will hear the penetrating whistles of the red-winged black birds, the pleasant calls of the bobwhites and the familiar melody of a song sparrow. Your eyes will follow the aerial circus of the barn swallows as they swoop and circle, climb and dive. A hawk may slowly float in wide circles overhead and a frog go ker-plunk in the nearby creek.

But in a few minutes you will begin to hear the sweet, subdued meadow music of the smaller forms of life. There are some 800,000 known species of insects on our planet, and a score of them are likely within yards of you. Look down among the grasses to the small flowering plants; watch the plump gold and black bumblebees and listen as they drone leisurely by on their search for nectar and pollen. Golden-banded honeybees are out in force on a warm sunny day; grasshoppers take off from hidden landing fields and circle in the sunlight with a softly-burred, whirring sound.

When the June dusk darkens the meadows and moves slowly down eastern slopes of hills, the plaintive, oddly stirring cries of the whippoorwill sound through the darkness. It is probable that for every person who has seen this unusual bird, hundreds of others have only heard its poignant call. It belongs to the group known as goatsuckers, for a European legend says it sucked milk from goats. Man has always feared forms of life that move silently in the darkness, and so it is with this bird of harsh scientific name: *Antrostomus vociferus*.

It is a chunky, square-fronted bird, about the size of a robin, but it has long, tapering wings which make it seem larger. It has very small feet and usually perches sideways on fence rails and limbs. It swoops and swerves through the air, not very high above ground, gathering night-flying insects in its large, bristle-fringed mouth. The black-gray-white mottled bird is difficult to see at dusk. Two eggs, grayish-white with lilac streaks, are laid on the ground, frequently on leaves near a shrub, log, or stone.

When night has curtained off the distant hills and the sunset glow in the west has faded, the whippoorwill sits on the fence and calls to the twinkling stars and the waxing slice of moon. There are nights in late spring and early summer when the bird cries by the hour; occasionally it will sing the night through. Some think the call is lonely and sad, but it wouldn't be June unless the calls, "whippoorwill, whippoorwill," were sounding in the darkness.

Have you heard the deep-throated, bass notes that come from sloughs and ponds on a moist, warm night? If one uses the word frog, the great majority think immediately of bullfrogs. Few persons know there are many kinds of frogs in eastern North America, including such interesting varieties as the cricket frog, the bird-voiced tree frog, the barking frog, the meadow frog, the ornate chorus frog, the squirrel-tree frog, the pickerel frog, and the wood frog.

Frogs are amphibians, an animal class which stands between gilled and finned creatures and the lunged and limbed group. When the sonorous, rhythmic notes of the bullfrog are heard, there is something strangely appealing and haunting in the deep-pitched music. It is never hurried; there is no tension, no sense of forcing. The throaty, husky tones blend with the darkness shutting off the hills and valleys.

The bullfrog, *Rana catesbiana*, resembles a creature from another world. He's the monarch of the frog kingdom, enormous in size, massive, patriarchal. He has huge, bulging eyes, and he makes me think of an elderly man-of-the-world who regards the human race with amused tolerance and kindly skepticism. There is a band of gleaming gold around the pupils of his eyes and another around the outer margin. Beneath those protruding eyes there is the wide mouth, fixed in a permanent grin. A full-grown bullfrog is often seven or eight inches long, and some frogs weigh as much as five pounds or even more. Most of the time, the bullfrog floats at his ease with only his head above water. When occasion requires, he can move with surprising speed, not only in the water but on land. Once in a while he climbs onto dry land, and in an emergency he makes leaps that carry his bulk five feet or more through the air.

The breeding and life cycle of the bullfrog is as fascinating as his appearance. In the spring, the female emerges from winter hibernation in the mud, mates, and lays from 15,000 to 20,000 eggs in a gelatinous film. I have seen films that were a foot or more in length and width. The eggs hatch in a week to two weeks, depending probably on the temperature of the water. When a bullfrog tadpole is a fortnight old, it has a big head and tiny tail. Tadpoles live on algae and other small plants in the water.

Most people think bullfrog tadpoles change to frogs during the first summer, but with bullfrogs it takes three to four years before they reach maturity. The first fall, the bullfrog tadpole is five or six inches long, and it goes into winter hibernation in the mud as a tadpole. The second spring, the hind legs start growing, but the long tail is kept for weeks. Then, in the middle summer, the front legs break through; the left front leg comes first. Slowly the tail is taken into the body and provides food for the period during which the tadpole cannot eat. By September of the second summer, the spectacular metamorphosis is finished. But the bullfrog does not reach maturity until the next year, or occasionally the fourth summer.

Old "jug-o-rum" is king of the frogs, the monarch of all he surveys. When the bullfrog's chorus gets under way, the ancient melody accentuates the peace of the countryside.

Weeding

Naturally a sensible citizen is not going to continue the fight against weeds all summer long, any more than he will keep battling dandelions and crabgrass in his lawn after a few weeks of token fighting in the spring. I have learned that if weeds can be kept in reasonable control until mid-July, the rest of the season matters very little. Crops will mature if they get a good head start, and as far as I can discover a reasonable number of weeds do not seriously reduce the crop. At least the law of diminishing returns functions sufficiently so that weeding is not demonstrably profitable.

However, in the early part of the season, weeding is necessary. I have experimented considerably with weeding techniques over the years. You can bend over from the waist, which is beneficial to the waistline, but after half an hour it generates a severe strain on leg muscles. The next position is to kneel on one knee and progress in an awkward hitch-and-jerk fashion. This is satisfactory for a spell but hard on the hip joints. Eventually a middle-aged, generously girthed man comes to it. He gets down on both knees; he leans forward on his elbows; his posterior is high and his head low. The family makes humorous comments and occasionally snaps a candid photo, but you can work with both hands and maintain a good rate of speed. Weeding is essential, one assumes, and that's the price a man pays for a successful garden. But it is always a rewarding day when you can go out, survey the garden, and conclude that from now on the plants can take care of themselves.

When I was a boy, it seemed to me that the vegetable least able to take care of itself was the turnip. Turnips vary widely in quality, not only in sweetness, but in the caliber of the root; but a topflight turnip is a good vegetable, especially when it is turned into flavorful cream of turnip soup, baked turnip fluff, turnip stew, and turnip croquettes fried in bacon fat.

Theoretically, the mechanical turnip planter was supposed to deposit a seed every six inches in the furrows; but somehow the turnips seemed to be about three inches apart, and every two or three feet something went wrong and several seeds were planted close together. "Thin 'em out," Father would say, "so they will be just about one foot apart. That way we'll have good big turnips come October."

I worked along row by row through the hot afternoon hours. I used the hoe whenever I could, but I usually had to get down on my knees to thin by hand where the plants were thick. No use dawdling, for what I didn't do that day I would have to do the next. The only thing was to keep plugging along, waiting for the clock in the village steeple to strike four. Then I knew I could quit, get my swim in the meadow brook and cool off before going for the cows.

On an especially hot day when I was weeding the garden or thinning turnips, it was a powerful morale booster to know that in the shade of nearby shrubs there was an earthern jug of switchel. Most boys and girls today have never heard of switchel, and in competition with soda fountain and bottled pop, it might not win a popularity prize. But my grandfather always claimed that while you were weeding, haying, or harvesting, there was nothing to equal a long drink of cool, tangy switchel to keep work going at full speed.

Mother's formula was a gallon of water, two cups of sugar, a cup of molasses, a cup and a quarter of vinegar, and a teaspoon of ginger. Occasionally she put in a handful of rolled oats. Once in a while for a pleasant, subtle, flavor change, she used brown sugar instead of white.

The big, gray, earthenware jug was kept on the dirt cellar floor overnight so it would be cool. During the day, menfolk were careful to keep it in the shade or beneath a haycock. When a young fellow was working along in the garden, he could go to the jug every so often for a short drink. It was better, he thought, to take a little at frequent intervals. It broke the monotony of the work, and of course along the hedgerow, it was always possible to spend a few minutes hunting for a woodchuck hole or searching for a hornet's nest. We do not expect that switchel will return to favor, but we wish all boys could know the pleasant, tangy, thirst-quenching goodness of this old-fashioned drink.

First Mess of Peas

There was a time when a forehanded farmer could plant his peas in early April and be certain of a good mess along about the third week in June. I am always careful of dissipating undue energy, so I like to grow my peas on a permanent trellis and do my picking standing up.

A good farmer considers the first mess of peas almost an annual ritual. He is glad to go to the garden with the womenfolk and pick the pods from the tall vines. He presses open a few pods, runs his thumb along, and eats a few peas just to taste the sweet, delicate flavor.

After the peas are picked, it is evident that someone must do the shelling. The best method devised to date is to place an old, comfortable, wicker chair in the shade of a tree by the garden wall. Hold the pan of peas in the lap; discard the pea pods into an old pail at the side. Sitting comfortably in the shade you can work along, listening to the song sparrows and catbirds.

The first mess of peas should always be a supper dish. A perspicacious citizen always serves them the same way. Open two fluffy white biscuits in a soup plate. Lather the four halves with butter, and then over them pour a full pint of peas with plenty of hot, fragrant juice. That is the way to eat fresh green peas, no more than half an hour from vine to table. That is why the first mess of peas is a special event in the garden harvest.

The Flowers of June

Hundreds of species of plants belong to the vast composite family of herbs. An herb, botanically, is any succulent stem plant; for the word applies to more than Grandmother's dill, savory, thyme, marjoram, basil, and rosemary. The black-eyed Susan is a handsome, extrovertish, upstanding flower of the aster group; the stems are long and wiry, the deep yellow petals contrast strikingly with the dark, madder-purple discs, and the tiny florets create an appealing golden circle when their pollen is "ripe."

Most of our immigrant flowers and weeds have traveled westward, but not this independent plant. The black-eye has fought its way from west to east. Decades ago, western farmers began shipping clover seed eastward and seeds of the black-eye came with it. The plant delights in dry fields, upland pastures, and dusty roadsides; it holds its own through long dry spells along with oxeye daisies and wild carrots. The black-eye is a summer flower that blends well with blue skies, hot weather, and white clouds.

Botanically, the flower is especially interesting. The nectar is deep in the florets' tubes and can be taken only by an insect with a long slender tongue. But the pollen stamens at the fringe of flower heads hold their golden grains for bees and wasps, butterflies, and beetles. Only flying insects can eat at this free lunch-counter, for nature long ago developed a dense growth of tiny bristles on the stems to repel creeping insects. The black-eye, Maryland's state flower, is just an everyday flower of the hot weather season, but if you will study one carefully and examine the blossom under a hand lens, you will see both beauty and symmetry in an interesting plant that helps make this a flowering world.

Country children hold buttercups beneath each other's chins, and if there is yellow reflection, it indicates a liking for butter. Few native flowers have been so much written about as the common meadow buttercup. Pliny thought that buttercups grew where frogs thrived, so he gave the name *Ranunculaceae* to the family. The field buttercup, most prominent member of the family, is *Ranunculus*, "little frog." The buttercup group is also called the "crowfoot" because the deeply cleft segments resemble the foot of the big, black bird. Pliny also wrote that if one eats the buttercup, it will stir him to exuberant laughter; and he gave the further advice that unless one washes his buttercup down with "pineapple kernels and pepper dissolved in date wine," he may laugh himself from this world into the next.

Other ancient writers claimed that one species of buttercup furnished poison for arrows. But the buttercup is a friendly, everyday flower, and like all simple, fundamentally true things, it is cherished. The bright yellow blossoms add interest to the meadow, although a farmer does not like the buttercup in his hay any more than he does the scarlet devil's paintbrush. Still and all, buttercups are the ancestors of all other common flowers, and there is something of ancient dignity and timeless simplicity as the yellow blossoms reflect the gold of June's sun.

JULY

SOFT COLORS PAINT THE HILLS AT DAWN AND LAYERS OF gray mist hover over the meadows. Cobwebs gleaming with beads of dew make geometrical patterns on the grass. There's a brooding sense of fulfillment as the sun climbs into the sky. It is summer now, and the days begin their gradual descent. The dawn chorus is ended; hedgerows and gardens are filled with the flutterings of young birds. Rows of green cover the brown soil, and a countryman checks his corn to see that it is knee high. Potatoes hold masses of white blossoms above their green leaves, and out in the hillside orchard, apples are the size of golf balls.

Brooks trickle quietly down from the highlands; the larger streams in the meadow flow unhurriedly along. Kingfishers sit like statues in the willows above the pools and high in the sky a hawk rides the wind in graceful circles. Barn swallows swoop and dive in their dawn to dusk search for food. Nature is settling down to the quiet period of growth that leads to the time of harvest.

This is the month of heat. The feeding rootlets of billions of grasses, shrubs, and trees take liquid to the leaves, where the magic of light manufactures food for the young plants. Along the pasture walls, sumac holds out chunky candles on scraggly candelabra; and down in the swales, the slender, grown heads of cattails stand erect among the reeds and coarse grasses. Around the garden edges, milkweed blossoms offer a rich, nectar harvest for insects; and on thin-soiled pasture hillsides, pink spires of steeple-jack splash color against the sunbrowned grass.

This is the heart of summer. Through the long, hot days you can feel the progress of the maturing year. There may be a long period of dry, searing weather as farmers watch for signs of needed rain. Or black thunderheads may billow from the horizon, and while jagged lightning illuminates the sky, heavy rain may drench the land. Nature seems to balance its extremes and life goes on. Summer is the time of growth. A man who went forth to plant a few weeks ago can now look forward to the harvest.

Picking Potato Bugs

Every citizen should experience certain fundamental activities in his younger years. One early summer activity with a solid tradition is picking potato bugs by hand and dropping them into a can partially filled with coal oil. We take the starchy tubers for granted, but this plant of the nightshade family has an interesting history. Potatoes were discovered by the Spaniards in Central America and sent to Europe; not, as many erroneously believe, introduced into this country in 1717 by a group from northern Ireland which settled in Londonderry, New Hampshire. Potatoes were grown in the Atlantic colonies before this.

Commercial growers do not depend upon hand labor today; the entire process is mechanized. But a generation and more ago, farm boys dropped the seed by hand. It was a farm lad's work to hoe once or twice before the rows were hilled. Then came the potato bugs and Father would say one morning when he had finished his piece of pie, "Son, better pick potato bugs today."

It wasn't a bad job at all, much better than cleaning out calf pens or hoeing corn. With can in hand, I walked up and down the rows picking the handsomely colored, black-and-yellow striped beetles from the green leaves. I would not necessarily call it an exciting task, but if the potato patch were located some distance from the house and away from the sharp observation of sisters who felt a moral obligation to check on my activities, there were a few interesting side trips that could be made. There were woodchuck holes to explore with Shep; there were big, cone-shaped hornets' nests in the gray birches by the pasture wall. Sometimes a big black snake would be sunning itself on a flat boulder at the field's edge. And there was always the possibility of having a conversation with a chipmunk.

So far as a chipmunk is concerned, walls and fences were invented for him. He likes to be reasonably close to human beings, but feels he has the right to scold if persons come too close. He is a debonair, friendly fellow in his striped coat and bushy tail that floats behind as he dashes about his business.

A chipmunk is widely traveled in a small area, for an acre or two is a chipmunk's world. He digs his tunnel down sharply for a few inches, slopes it gently for another two or three feet, and then levels off below the frost line. He excavates several food storage rooms and a nest room of leaves for the long winter sleep. Mating is in late winter; the four or five young are born in thirty-two days.

Mr. Chipmunk always looks frantically busy, feeding on the fruits and seeds of many plants. He isn't averse to a few June bugs, wire worms, and cutworms, either. And occasionally he takes unhatched eggs or small birds from nests. Why does the chipmunk stop, look, and listen so often? Because from the day he emerges from his underground birthplace, he faces enemies: cats, dogs, snakes, owls, foxes, and weasels.

Most people find the chipmunk more appealing than the red or gray squirrel. Busy as he is, he always has a moment to pass the time of day. Picking potato bugs was a pleasant occupation with a chipmunk keeping me company from his perch on the garden wall.

Berries

Once you could get large, flavorful, dead-ripe blackberries in the market, but farmers have given up raising this bramble. Cultivated blackberries have begun to take their place, even though, in my opinion, they have less flavor than the wild variety.

There is an art to picking wild blackberries on a late July day when you are caught up on the farm work and want to get off by yourself for a few hours. Needle-pointed blackberry spikes are strong and engender respect, so you should wear heavy overalls and jumper. Fasten a pail beneath a suspender button so you can pick with both hands, and then work your way into the dense tangle of vines by turning round and round as you move forward.

It is work, of course. But on a sultry day, when the mountains are dark green across the valley, it is a pleasant task to strip the dead-ripe berries from the vines. You should not let your mind wander too far from the job at hand, but in late afternoon as you amble down through the sugar grove and across the pasture, it doesn't do any harm to think about a delicious blackberry cobbler, with feather-light biscuits and plenty of heavy cream.

When it comes to blueberries, there seems to be a difference of opinion between the highbush versus the lowbush varieties. But I cast my vote for the highbush. There is no question that they have a whiffle more flavor than the lowbush; they make better pies, puddings and muffins. And besides, it is more fun to pick standing up than to crawl around on sensitive knees.

It is good for a man to take time off to go blueberrying. In the right location the tall bushes are laden with fruit; you do not have to move around much to gather a generous harvest. At a swamp's edge or the low end of a pasture on a sun-bright summer's day, you can work along, filling your pail, and pause to listen to the complaining calls of young crows from the woodland or watch a hawk circling the sky on motionless wings. It may be that a brood of partridges will come wandering by or a big black snake will slither unhurriedly away.

Of course, a man is glad to take home a big pail of the blue nuggets for juicy pies and sweet cobblers. But when day is done and he heads for the house, he knows he has harvested something for the heart that is worth more than the fruit in his pail.

Rain on the Roof

Each season has its typical rains: cold, dreary rains in autumn; lashing sheets in winter, gentle rains in spring. Along in July when there has been a spell of drought for days or sometimes weeks, there is a rain that means much to those who live intimately with nature. The countryman can tell when it is coming. Hushed are the sounds of the countryside and the fields lie quiet and waiting. Thicker grows the cloud blanket and deeper the gray of its color. No movement of air stirs leaf or branch. The days have been hot and dry under the July sun. Brooks that leaped down from the highlands in spring are trickles of muted water; streams in rich-soil valleys flow lazily along. The hillsides have become parched in the drought; grasses have changed from green to amber and painted a neutral background for the red-purple spires of hardhack. The roadside trees are dusty and seared; the leaves on the elms that arch above peaceful village streets are dull green.

Gradually the change begins. Through the hot, brassy heat of a July day, the haze in the heavens begins to thicken. Hesitant breezes that come with a dry spell pull back, and the countryside waits. Birds hush their singing and the insects are silent. There is no rustle among the corn leaves and the tall elms in the meadows are still. Woodland ponds are smooth and no fish breaks the mirror surface. Minute by minute the sky darkens. Last loads of hay have been rushed to the scaffold and a man stands in the barn doorway and watches as the first drops begin to fall. Miniature geysers of dust rise as the drops hit the earth in the dooryard.

There are many kinds of rain and each has its own melody. Sometimes it is a gentle, low-pressure rain with small drops; sometimes there are harder, persistent rains with bigger drops. In autumn we are likely to get two or three wild windy gales when the rain comes in driving gusts, and in the night you can lie and listen to the drumming on the roof. The wind moans and groans around the northwest corner of the house and a blustery September storm often sounds like a wailing January blizzard. Half a century ago, when the hard rains came and the wind blew, I could hear the voices of the storm wail in the chimney near my bed and the lashing of tree branches against the house.

There are many pleasant sounds in country living and each man has his favorite. I like the calls of the first robins in March when the fields are still patched with snow. I enjoy the soft music of a meadow in July when myriad small insects' wings produce a low-pitched, pleasant hum. There is joy in the song of a rose-breasted grosbeak at dawn as it sits on the top spike of a tall pine and its husky carol floats down to the house. There is poignant satisfaction in the haunting song of the hermit thrush when at day's end it pours its liquid notes into a quiet, darkening world.

But perhaps because I am a countryman who likes to garden, my first vote goes to the steady, gentle rain after a prolonged period of drought. Since boyhood days, I have known the importance of weather. I can remember that when we had a good apple crop on the way, Father would anxiously scan the summer skies for signs of rain.

Those who live intimately with nature and are concerned with grasses, crops and trees always watch for signs of rain. After a drought, the gentle drumming of rain on the roof is welcome music. It is the right kind of a rain, steady and soft, that will soak down to the waiting roots.

A Tree That Stands Alone

You see them in the lowlands, along the fences and walls of mowing fields, on boulder-studded pasture hillsides and on craggy ridge heights. A tree that stands alone is a symbol. Graceful elms along the rivers and brooks, patriarchal beeches, great oaks and gaunt maples are trees that have fought a long, testing battle and have established their strength.

For a century and more they have known the tempests of winter, the miracle of spring, and the heat of summer. A century ago a small seed found sanctuary in good soil and a tiny white root struck downward; a slender green shoot lifted toward the sky and stars. Over the decades while the nation fought wars and grew in power, the trees grew taller. Cattle have rested in their shade; birds have made homes among their branches. Great roots reached deep into the earth to find food as bole and branches developed.

Every man who loves trees and thinks of them as friends has his own favorite species. Some think the evergreens loveliest; some prefer the beauty of the white birch; others like sugar maples, white oaks, or the vase-like elms. I dislike choosing one above all others, but if a choice must be made, I would give first place to an old, scraggly beech. Since ancient days, the beech has been beloved by man. Theocritus wrote, "I ran to meet you as a traveler rests from the sun under a shady beech," and Virgil said, "No wars did men molest when only beechen bowls were in request."

You no longer see extensive forests of beeches with tautly smooth bark and widely spreading branches. Time was, three centuries ago, when gray beeches stretched mile after mile along rich river valleys, over gently rolling hills and across upland plateaus. Even a hundred years ago, there were great forests of these trees where wild pigeons came by the hundreds of thousands to eat the nuts, and where farmers pastured their hogs in autumn to fatten on the sweet mast.

Throughout the changing seasons, the gray beech has a dignified beauty. In winter, the slender, pointed buds are a rich, glowing brown; in spring, there are attractive pollen-bearing and seed-bearing blossoms as the leaves are starting; and after the first hard, black frosts of October, the smooth nuts begin dropping from the spiny husks.

One of the most appealing pictures of the countryside to a tree-lover is a solitary, gnarled beech standing in a field or on a sidehill. A tree that stands alone represents qualities that a man admires. The tree has met and conquered the storms of life; it has bowed but never broken before powerful forces. Its roots are in the ground but its head is lifted to the light.

Cherries

The cherry is one of the best fruits, and I regret that technically it is called a drupe. That word does not do justice to the tart deliciousness of plump, sour cherries, correctly blended with spice and sugar and protected by two crusts of topflight quality.

All cherries are descended from the wild cherry and the extent of their improvement is indicated by the number of birds that are anxious to help harvest the crop. The problem is that robins and waxwings enjoy cherries as much as I do. They have an uncanny ability to wait until the morning when I say, "Mother, I'll pick some cherries today if you'll bake a cherry pie for dinner." Then I go to the cherry tree behind the woodshed and find that the birds were up early and got there before me. I've tried various devices to frighten them away. I hang glass jars among the branches; I string strips of white cloth; I drape a length of black rubber hose which I hope resembles a snake. Nothing seems to do much good, so I am resigned to sharing my cherries with the birds, and hope they feel the same way about me. Perhaps the solution is to have at least two sour-cherry trees, one for the birds and one to provide the necessary fruit for pies, puddings, and a few quarts to freeze and can.

With that many cherries, you naturally need a cherry stoner to fasten to the kitchen table. The cherry stoner I used as a boy was described succinctly in the mail-order catalog. "This Perfect Cherry Stoner does not crush the cherry or cause any loss of juice; a perfect machine for large, small, or Californian cherries. The seed extracting knife drives the seed into one dish and actually throws the cherry into another. The marks of the knife can scarcely be seen on the seeded fruit. It seeds from 20 to 30 quarts per hour. No grinding, no mashing; no loss of juice. Heavily tinned to prevent rust. Price each—60 cents."

It certainly was not hard work to push down on the knife that eliminated the seed. Some cherry juice spattered on the table and floor, to be sure, but as the big kettle was gradually filled, a fellow kept in mind the cherry puddings and pies that were to come.

Mother usually planned to can at least twenty-five quarts for winter use. "Nothing like a cherry pie in January to keep a man's courage up," Father would say on a below-zero, blizzardy night when a hot cherry pie appeared for supper. It isn't necessary for the average family to grow its own cherries today when you can buy good fruit canned, frozen, or fresh. But I strongly feel that something should be done to foster more cherry pies. Surely a girl who can learn to run a modern stove with its supersonic devices, gongs, whistles, sirens, stop clocks, alarms, multiple timing devices and jet-powered contraptions is capable of mastering the technique of making a good cherry pie.

Springhouse

A dependable spring has always been cherished by those who have lived on farms. Sometimes the springhouse was built over a running cold water brook, but whether spring or stream, the small house was a sanctuary to a fourteen-year-old on a hot summer day. In a scooped-out place, often lined with bricks or flat rocks, milk and cream cans sat until the cream was ripe for churning. In the cool dimness, left-over dishes of food were kept between meals. Long before man conceived the miracle of electric refrigeration and the magic of home freezers, the humble springhouses, built of wood and clay, brick, or a combination of materials, were serving the nation's farm and village homes.

In hot weather, butter was churned in the springhouse. Here the eggs were kept and the dressed chickens hung on Friday evening to cool out until they were put in the oven for Sunday dinner when relatives from neighboring towns gathered for a family party. On a hot day after a load of hay had been pitched off and stored away in the blistering heat of the scaffold, it was pleasant to stop a few minutes in the cool, moist air of the springhouse and drink a cupful or two of cold, tangy buttermilk and lunch on a few of Mother's cookies.

Haying

A few years ago haying was a touch-and-go period of the farm year. Good farmers with heavy crops of timothy and clover watched the weather signs because it took at least two days for heavy hay to "make." A lad who drove the big team on the mowing machine in the morning, drove one of the horses on the hayrake in the afternoon. The hay was usually cocked for the night and then spread out the next forenoon for the rest of the curing. Sometimes when the hay was especially heavy, the tedder was used, and the steel tines tore the grasses apart to speed the drying.

Father or the hired man usually pitched on and someone

had to tramp and build the load on the hayrack. A fourteen-year-old's job was to pull the bullrake—sometimes called the "loafer" —an implement used to rake up the scatterings. It was six or seven feet wide with teeth approximately a foot in length. The handles came together at the front, and spread at the rear to the ends of the big rake.

The bulk of the raking was done by the iron horserake with its trip catch, leaving windrows of hay that were pulled into cocks. Around the walls and fences, posts and trees, a lad used a regular hand rake. But when it came time to load on, it was the bullrake a lad pulled, hustling to keep up with the man who was pitching on.

There are favorable points about a bullrake. It is wide and covers territory fast; with tall uprights at the rear of the teeth, you can accumulate a good-sized load. But along with these two constructive points, there is one pertinent fact. The long pointed teeth of the bullrake were always in dangerous proximity to a boy's heels. When you were working at top speed, especially when black thunderheads were billowing up from the horizon and Father was rushing to get the sweet-smelling clover and timothy under cover before the storm broke, the bullrake had a perverse habit of catching on hummocks. If the first tentative pull did not free the teeth, a lad was likely to give a hard, purposeful yank, and the rake would leap forward and catch him a sharp blow just above the heel.

Pitching off in the barn and storing the hay on the hot scaffold was not a very pleasant job either. Under the eaves of a barn on a hot July day, the sweat poured down your face and the hay chaff itched all over. But in the kitchen that night while you waited for your turn in the tin tub, you had the feeling of a job well done.

I feel that some of that feeling of accomplishment is gone now that mechanical power has taken over the harvest. Do you recall how proud Grandfather was of his ability to mow with snath and scythe? And perhaps you can still hear the ringing, metallic notes as he stood the snath on end, pulled a whetstone from his overall pocket and touched up the cutting edge of his scythe.

It is true that farmers had horse-drawn mowing machines in the days when fringe-top surreys were still on the roads, but many farms had a low area at one end of a field or a meadow where the soil was too soft for the horses. Mowing with a scythe is an art and Grandfather was a master craftsman. "Keep the heel down," he would say to a lad who was trying to master the craft. "Keep the heel down and take easy, swinging strokes. Don't try to cut too much at one swing. Remember, easy does it." It was poetry in motion to watch him. Unhurriedly, rhythmically, the blade swung back and forth, and at each cutting stroke the tall coarse grass fell over smoothly. At each stroke, there was faint, whispering music as the razor-edged scythe sheared off the stems; at each stroke Grandfather edged forward a few inches, and the double track of his feet made a narrow path in the lush, heavy grass.

Men still use scythes in swampy places; they still trim out around fences and walls and trees. But each year the music of the scythes grows less; each year mechanization and reallotment of land changes the farming scene. But still in some places the notes of whetstone on steel bring back boyhood memories.

Tin Peddler

We recently read that the tin peddler is staging a come-back. But with today's modern, high-speed trucks, I doubt that the arrival of a covered vehicle behind a gasoline engine would have the thrill that farm children knew in the early 1900s era. In those days the tin peddler came once a year to our farm and his annual visit was an exciting, anticipated event.

Children saw him coming far down the road, and by the time Old John arrived, Father, Mother, the hired man, and all the children were waiting for the small friendly man, the chunky horses with their shining harnesses and the big, bright red van. Unless farm work was very pressing, the rest of the day except for barn chores was a special holiday. Old John we called him, because we could not pronounce his long name with the many consonants. Years ago John had come to this country for a new start, after one of the tragic, inhuman feuds that periodically flared in southeastern Europe. At that time he had lost his wife and children, his parents and many friends.

Old John always put up for the night at the farm. After supper he spread beautiful laces, satins and silks, jewelry, pots and pans and baskets on the big kitchen table. After Mother and my sisters had made their choices, Old John tucked his beloved violin under his chin, and there in the farm kitchen we listened while his wonderful music laughed and cried and danced. The poignant, minor-key melodies soared to sweet, thin high notes, and then the violin whispered haunting stories among the low notes. In the soft golden glow of kerosene lamps, we listen to the gypsy music tell of life in a strange and far-off land.

The Rooster

When young roosters exercise their querulous voices at the first faint tinge of daylight, a man sometimes wonders why they get up so early. Shakespeare called the rooster "the trumpet of the morn" and also "the bird of dawning." With endorsement like that, a man has to be reasonable about this farm problem. There is no question that a rooster has a constitutional right to sound off, the same as a congressman or a traffic policeman.

And roosters have their good points, too. *The New England Farmer* of September, 1861, put it succinctly. "The rooster is of great consequence in the hen yard. He talks to the hens, helps them to select their nests, sympathizes with them in all their troubles, settles all their differences, calls them to meals, and protects them from their enemies." An adult rooster is a noble bird. He struts with assurance and poise; he governs with benevolent paternalism.

A man should be patient with young roosters, even though he wishes they would wait a spell before beginning to practice. Probably the most intelligent attitude is one of scientific curiosity. If you listen carefully day by day, you can detect a gradual and steady improvement in the technique, volume and musical quality. When a young human being begins to practice on a saxophone, violin, or flute, the results call for patience and understanding. Perhaps we should adopt the same attitude when young roosters start practicing their dawn music.

Horseradish

Consider the subject of horseradish. There are few scenes in family life more touching than a group of womenfolk weeping together as they prepare this wiry white root for preserving. When a man sees tears coursing down his wife's cheeks, he knows he will have his favorite horseradish condiment to use on corned beef and baked beans for months to come. *Amoracia lapathifolia* is a doughty enemy, but in spite of its tear-producing power, good housewives should do their duty.

I can recall the heartening, wholesome picture when Mother and my three sisters sat by the old drop-leaf cherry table in the kitchen and had a good, uninhibited crying jag. In the old days on the family farm, we had a tremendous bed of vigorous horseradish plants. The drain from the kitchen sink ran out behind the house; the water was carried from the house some twenty-five feet in a V-shaped wooden trough. Just beyond the trough, the horseradish bed flourished. All season long the rich, black soil was moist. I wasn't very fond of horseradish in those days but near the horseradish bed, there was a wonderful spot for me to dig worms.

The horseradish roots varied in size from big, bulky affairs to short, stubby ones, and long, slender, tapering ones. It was my job to dig up the roots, wash them and trim off the scraggly ends. Then it was up to the womenfolk. With tears flowing, they sliced the roots very thin, and then put them on the shelf behind the kitchen stove to dry. When the slices were completely dry, they were ground in a mortar and sealed in a jar. The dry powder was then ready to sprinkle on roast pork or roast beef to sharpen up the taste.

Horseradish also had other admirable qualities. If you had a freckle problem, one old book advised you to "grate a fresh horseradish root very fine, cover with fresh buttermilk, and let stand overnight. Strain through cheesecloth, and wash the face night and morning with the resulting liquor." The book also added: "Milk as a cosmetic maybe improved by infusing in it freshly grated horse radish. This is wonderful for slight discolorations or eruptions of the skin."

In the event you plan to start a horseradish bed, I should warn you that this perennial herb spreads very rapidly. So far as I know, it does not mature seeds in our climate, although it produces purplish sepals and white petals. More than half the nation's production of this plant is in the St. Louis, Missouri, region. The soil is well adapted to its growth—deep and well-drained. Settlers from Europe began to grow the root, and for about a century now horseradish has been an important crop in this region. Cuttings are used to start a new bed, as we use divisions of rhubarb.

I feel that most farmers and many suburban gardeners should have at least a small bed of this root crop. We need more family unity and more tasks that bind a family together. Can you think of anything that better proves family togetherness than a group of women sitting around a kitchen, weeping and wiping their eyes while grinding or grating horseradish?

Sir Christopher Wren

Physical size is not a valid criterion of a man's abilities and the same observation holds true for birds. One should not downgrade the house wren because of its five-inch length and small body. Sir Christopher is a valiant scrapper as well as a gallant gentleman. He arrives before his mate in the spring, bursts forth intermittently all day long with a bubbling trill, and between arias starts to build one or more nests.

The female wren is particular and is reported on occasion to throw out the construction work of Sir Christopher and to start all over. I have never seen this, but I have watched many remodel, refurbish, and add material to the nest. I suppose they feel that most males are somewhat inept and blundering when it comes to housekeeping.

The female lays from six to nine tiny, pink-gray eggs that are splashed and streaked with purple and brown. When the eggs hatch, the male pitches in and helps feed the brood; but even while the young birds are developing, he frequently takes time out to sound his enthusiastic trill.

House wrens are good friends and neighbors. They feed

almost entirely on various kinds of insects. We commonly think of house wrens as modest, pleasant, dun-colored little birds that continue to make music even in the hot weather of July and August. I am not saying that all citizens should emulate Sir Christopher. Still, if a man would remember to sing a bit as he does his daily chores, it might make the wheels go round more smoothly.

Fourth of July

Do you remember that thrilling, long-anticipated Fourth of July half a century ago? Remember how you saved pennies, nickels, and dimes for fire crackers, sparklers, and Roman candles? Remember how you sneaked downstairs, went around under your sisters' bedroom window and sacrificed one of your cannon crackers to start the day? And when your sisters complained to Father, he smiled and said, "Well, it's a little early but after all, it's Fourth of July and a boy has some rights." From then on, it was a question of spacing your ammunition so it would last during a long day.

It was a big day for everyone, and somehow during the activities a lad caught a feeling of the meaning of the day. There was fun and excitement, but there was an underlying current that I think is missing today, a deep feeling for our country's history.

The Fourth always meant parades and speeches, picnics and band concerts. Each year at Town Meeting we appropriated money for the band. Every Saturday evening through the winter, men and boys in heavy boots and thick woolen pants gathered in the hall on the third floor of the village hotel for band practice. On the Fourth as you watched the men playing a spirited march tune or an old favorite, you could scarcely believe your eyes—or your ears. It hardly seemed possible it could be the same group.

The band played all summer long at the Wednesday evening band concerts, but the concert on the Fourth was its first chance to show what it could do. Men and boys were spruce and chipper. Blue uniforms with plenty of showy gold braid were freshly pressed; each man had a close haircut. Instruments gleamed in the sun. But to the eyes of a fourteen-year-old who hoped he would be in the band next year, the crowning glory was the magnificent cap. It was big; it was generously splashed with gold braid and a big gold eagle, and it had plenty of heavy white cord for ballast.

Before the concert began, families gathered in the pine grove behind John Hancock Grange, and picnicked among the pines on the bluff above Norway Pond. It was almost like a banquet as the food was spread on blankets and old quilts. Big boys set off cannon crackers on the shore of the pond, and mothers kept their eyes on small fry who liked to set off a string of their small crackers near an unsuspecting person. Then, while the sun slowly dipped behind the mountain and shadows began to fill the valley, the band played old and beloved melodies. When day was done and shadows dark, the village lamplighter climbed onto the bandstand and lit the kerosene lamps in front of their shining silvered reflectors.

In between full band numbers there were duets and quartets of brass and woodwinds, and always the crowd was generous with applause. And then along about nine, the band played "Goodnight, Ladies." As the sweet notes floated out on the evening air, the voices of hundreds of people joined in singing all three stanzas. The concert was over, and out along quiet country roads families rode homeward beneath bright stars that twinkled down from a blue-black velvet sky.

July Evening

Across the northern half of the nation on warm July evenings, farm families sit in wicker rocking chairs and enjoy the relaxing period of dusk. When day is done and the sun unhurriedly drops below the line of mountains, a man enjoys a quiet, peaceful period as the countryside tucks in for the night. A multitinted afterglow lingers in the sky; the colors change from bright to pastel and then to soft grays and blues. Shadows slowly creep down the hillsides, cross the brooding valleys and climb the eastern slopes.

For an hour the chimney swifts stage their evening aerial circus, circling, climbing and swooping earthward with effortless grace. A sleepy robin carols "goodnight" from the old Astrakhan tree by the hen house; one by one, stars break through the purple veil; a whippoorwill calls from the rail fence at the low end of the field. As dusk deepens, the chimney swifts settle in the house chimney with staccato twittering talk. Cowbells tinkle from the night pasture and the musical notes of the church clock in the village float by in the cooling air.

When darkness falls, fireflies stage their red-gold ballet, dancing close to the lawn or performing glowing movements high in the air. They may dance in close formation or they may separate and fling themselves away in whirling, angular flights. The red lines glow and fade in the darkness.

Fireflies breed near the ground surface and enjoy damp weather. Scientists have studied the light phenomenon for many years and still do not agree on the cause of the luminescence. There is a bright glow of light but no heat from the beetle of the family *Lampyridae*, from a Greek word meaning "glowworm." Some 1500 species of fireflies have been identified. Chemists tell us the light comes from a substance known as luciferin. But technicalities are not important on peaceful summer evenings when you sit on a porch and watch fireflies dance in the darkness. They are one of summer's most appealing sights.

The ideal chair for a summer evening on the front porch, in my opinion, is an old-fashioned rocker. In my time, I have tried many different chairs, some of which were acceptable. There is much to be said for a Morris chair with a back you can adjust. A big overstuffed chair has certain good points while you are in it; but some such chairs are so low-slung that a man consumes most of his restored energy in lifting himself to his feet.

All things considered, nothing has yet been invented which suits me as well as an old-fashioned wicker rocking chair. According to tradition, the first rocking chair was invented in the middle 1600's on the farm of a Deacon Brewster in Plymouth Colony. The mistress of the house was an invalid, and one of the farm hands with an inventive turn of mind figured a chair that would rock might be helpful. Thus the principle of the rocking chair was born.

A solid, correctly-built wicker rocking chair appeals to a man. It is soothing to nerves and muscles to move gently back

and forth on a warm July evening. Sitting and rocking, feeling
the magic of the night and listening to the mysterious whispers
that always seem to begin when daylight disappears, a man can
get caught up with himself.

AUGUST

AUGUST IS THE TIME OF QUIET WATERS. THE WATER MOVES slowly in meadow brooks, and woodland ponds are smooth blue jewels reflecting the blue of the eight-month sky. Pools in green meadows where vase-like elms stand above the thick-matted grasses lie like shining glass. Rarely does the kingbird sitting on a limb of a willow shatter the glistening surface. High on wooden mountainsides, high on boulder-studded uplands, the water comes from crystal springs. Far above the brooding lowlands and many hundreds of feet above the pasture and evergreen belt, high on the rock-laced ridges, you may suddenly see a bubbling spring that starts a small rivulet downward among the ferns and bracken.

In August, tall clumps of interrupted ferns lean over a woodland brook; dark-green, toothed woodferns hide gray-black decaying limbs; leather woodferns cluster around protuding rocks, and narrow beech ferns grow lushly in the shadows of large boulders. Polypods creep along the fissures of ledges; and near the upper edge where the sun strikes for several hours, the delicate, green-gold, hay-scented ferns wave in the bright light. Ferns are among the earth's humble plants, but their graceful symmetry is a green chain that links the present with the time when the earth was young.

August brings sticky heat, and muggy sultriness lies on the land like a half-wrung-out blanket. A brassy sun follows its trail across the sky, and the red of the sunset is a repetition of the red flares at dawn. The roadsides grow dusty, and the leaves lose their deep green hue. There is a different spirit when the year moves into the eighth month. Twice in that segment of time that brings a complete climatic cycle, nature pauses to consolidate its forces for the major change ahead. In February and again in August, you can feel the brooding expectancy.

August dawns are moist and fog fingers hover in the river valleys. Lawns are spangled with cobwebs, and the dewy grass is wet on a boy's bare feet as he drives the cows to pasture. Dew is moisture that forms in the night. In some hot climates, there is sufficient dew to take the place of rain. Down through the centuries man has used the word as a symbol of purity and freshness. It derives from old Anglo-Saxon "deaw," and there are some who believe the word "dew" is the most beautiful in our language. In the Bible one finds reference to it—meaning blessing or good; "the golden dew of sleep" is from Shakespeare. Many writers have spoken of dew "falling," but the gleaming drops of liquid on intricately woven spider webs, on strawberry and clover leaves, or spaced along a slender blade of grass were condensed from moisture in the air.

As the sun pulls into a pale blue sky, heat begins to press against the earth, and the dew quickly disappears. At high noon the landscape lies hot and seared. It may be true, as some people claim, that August is "tired summer," but there is strength enough left in the eighth month to come up with a blistering heat wave. Men who grow corn commercially, and the family gardener who is proud of his patch of sweet corn, don't object too strenuously. They know it takes hot days and warm nights to push maize to maturity. It isn't true that August is necessarily hotter than July, but as you will hear several times before fall coolness takes over, "It isn't the heat; it's the humidity."

The heat wave crawls across fields and meadows; it infiltrates woodlands and valleys. The temperature inches up toward the 100 mark and hour by hour the heat and humidity seem to thicken. Corn leaves curl in the bright sun and the soil in the garden cakes and splits. Tomatoes hang listlessly and the grasses on the uplands turn to amber and gold.

Noises die away as the heat wave presses its hot hand on the landscape. An occasional call comes from the woods where a young crow is trying its voice; a lackadaisical cricket fiddles intermittently beneath the farm kitchen window; a grasshopper takes off on a short, staccato flight. Perhaps for hours, perhaps for days, the searing temperature presses against the countryside.

Green Apples

Small boys and green apples have a natural affinity. It makes little difference that future citizens are repeatedly told that green apples are not worth their time. Each generation of men apparently prefers to make its own mistakes, and when green apples are beginning to swell, a twelve-year-old can be depended upon to investigate personally. It could be, of course, that a boy has heard his father orate at some length about a Porter apple pie made while the apples are still a trifle on the green side. Most countrymen consider themselves competent authorities on apple pies, and a man who has few opinions on other foods knows exactly what he wants in a pie—apples not quite ripe, rich flaky crust, plenty of spices, a teaspoon of molasses dribbled over the apple slices, and a few thin pieces of rat cheese on the side.

Green apples, truly green, are another matter, but a lad feels impelled to sample all the varieties as they ripen during the summer months. The acid tartness bites the tongue and crinkles the mouth. And sometimes, if a boy gets carried away, some peculiar things may begin to happen to his stomach. It is fitting that the apple is related to the rose and strawberry, both tops in their respective fields. A green apple is not comparable to a rosebud nor equal to a two-thirds ripe strawberry, but the unripe fruit on the bough is a promise of good things to come.

Woodland Waterfall

A woodland waterfall, where a clear, sandy-bottom brook falls two or three feet is a place of peace and beauty. Often there are moss-covered rocks that resemble cushions upholstered with rich green velvet. Sometimes bushes and shrubs crowd close to the singing water. Sometimes a waterfall is in open woodland, and the sound of the water blends with the music of the wind-moved branches.

Ferns like woodland waterfalls, and graceful fronds wave gently in moving air created by the falling water. Beads of moisture glisten on the foliage near the pool, and when the sun's rays strike through there are shafts of mullioned beauty. In the pool at the base of the waterfall, colored pebbles and varicolored stones send out rich, jewel-like glints.

In the heat of August, wildlife comes to the woodland pool. In the shallow water at pool's edge, vireos and warblers bathe at dusk. At dim-light dawn and again at dusk, deer come from the woodland, and a red fox stops by on his evening round to see if a frog is resting on the bank. Partridges come to the pool edge and in the soft, moist soil you may see the sharp footprints of the raccoon.

About this time of year, Father was likely to say to me, "Son, hitch Belle to the democrat and give the wheels a soaking in the brook passage." A brook passage was a wide, shallow pool beside a plank bridge where all four wheels could be in the water while the horse soaked summer-brittle hooves in the mud.

From time to time, I moved the horse and wagon forward or backward so that all of the rims and spoke ends would soak. In summer dryness, wooden rims shrank away from the steel, and spokes became loose. It was a long job, but that did not bother a twelve-year-old when he had a chance to explore the brook and plank bridge.

In bare feet, it was fun to edge along the mossy, cool rocks of the brook. Minnows flashed through the water, and sometimes one caught a glimpse of a trout or a water snake. It was even more fun to explore an old covered bridge by a waterfall. The old weather-stained, covered bridges are disappearing. Modern traffic needs a wider path; steel and cement are more efficient than wood. Even so about 2000 covered bridges are still in use today across the country.

Around the stove in country stores, men still argue as to why the bridges were covered, but that does not bother country boys who know the thrill of climbing along the outside wall if the bridge is the open, lattice-work type. Boys know the fun of scrambling into the overhead timbers and crawling the length of the bridge through dust and cobwebs. Many a man in a dignified city office can remember the fishing holes beneath covered bridges and the uneasy delight of edging cautiously along the slippery rocks of the abutment.

Advertising signs pasted on the outside planking described chewing tobacco, Wine of Life, spavin cures for horses, stallions at stud, liniments for beasts and man, farm machines, the circus and the county fair.

"Slow down or pay a two dollar fine," said one faded old sign. That is the basic message the old bridges have for men to-day, for they represent an era when life was slower and more flavorsome.

R.F.D.

Combinations of letters have become increasingly numerous and important in recent years; today it has reached the point where a list of all the alphabetical government agencies would probably paper the walls of a good-sized room—if the printing were small.

We would not wager more than a single August sweet that the average citizen can name more than a baker's dozen of these agencies that he helps to support. But we are sure of the fact that out on the countryside, everyone knows the meaning of R.F.D. Half a century ago, many men and women watched eagerly from farm dooryards until they saw the familiar horse and wagon coming along the dusty dirt road. For Tom Finch was more than the official representative of one of Uncle Sam's major departments; he was a friend who brought news of neighbors and carried messages to friends along the road.

The R.F.D. box was a humble, plebeian affair, set on a weathered post beside a country road. But from that box, letters went to relatives and friends in distant places; and through blizzards of winter and mud of spring, Tom brought the papers and magazines, letters and catalogs that were the living link with the outside world for the isolated homes on back country roads. The R.F.D. man was a friend to children and in his quiet way brought encouragement and cheer to many elderly persons who lived a lonesome life. We are not in favor of too many alphabetical combinations, but there is one that has proved itself. R.F.D. stands for something solid and good in the American way of life.

Getting the Cows

Do you remember when getting the cows was an eagerly anticipated part of the day's work? From time to time I read a piece in the farm press about the "zero pasture" program. In this system of farming, the cows do not go to pasture at all. They are kept confined in spacious yards; they have long, open sheds or pole barns in which to while away the time between milking.

We used a "green pasture" program on Glenrose Farm half a century ago. We had a typical New Hampshire pasture, and for a period in the spring after the cows were first turned out, the grass was lush and abundant. But as the summer came on, the grass gradually grew less abundant; and by mid-June, it was poor pasturage. That is why we, and most farmers in this section at least, always grew "green feed" for the milkers. Father was partial to oats, and always claimed that oats cut green before the lignin in the stems developed made excellent green feed. In the late afternoon, before I went for the cows, he would take a scythe and cut a small cartload to give the cows after milking.

I enjoyed the walk back across the meadow and through the pasture to the barway on the road from the house toward the village. I said our pasture was a typical one. It had open spaces, swamp areas, patches of evergreens, sandy knolls and bushy places. You could spend a pleasant half-hour checking fox dens and the swampy spot where muskrats built two or three domed houses each fall. And I always liked to look at the big stone pile at the lower end of the upland field to see if the big black snake was taking the sun.

Usually the cows were waiting at the gate, chewing their cuds and switching their tails. Sometimes at the height of fly time, they would stay in the evergreens to reduce the trouble with flies. The cows waited in order, for the caste system among cows is as rigid as the social order among hens and humans. For many years Buttercup was the undisputed leader. She was the first cow we bought on Glenrose Farm, and she governed like a blue-blooded arbiter of the social scene.

As soon as the bars were let down, Buttercup stepped sedately over them and led the procession up the sandy road to the barn. Rarely did I do anything except follow along. The cows knew that when they reached the barn they would get a measure of mixed cornmeal, middlings, bran, and ground oats. Sometimes we put a pint or so of molasses on the grain or hay. I suppose grain to a cow is the same as apple pie or chocolate bread pudding to us. Getting the cows was a responsibility I thoroughly enjoyed. I wish all of today's boys could know what it means to follow the cows home from pasture on an August evening.

Ladder and Basket Man

Approximately a century ago this nation was at the height of what we may logically call the wooden age. Craftsmen turned out uncounted numbers of wooden firkins, baskets and pails. Each town and village had its cooper who made flour, cider, and pork barrels. He also made sap buckets and buckets for wells; he made wooden milk pails and old-fashioned churns.

Much has been said in praise of the coopers and their products, but the ladder and basket men are not so well known. In August after haying was finished, farm families watched for Sam, who came along country roads with a huge two-horse framerack loaded with ladders and baskets. During the winter, spring, and early summer, Sam worked in his shop in Center Junction. He had a reputation for topflight ladders with cedar sides and white oak rounds; orchardists swore by Sam's workmanship for they needed a dependable ladder when picking or pruning in a twenty- to twenty-five-foot high tree. Sam made half-bushel picking baskets and strong bushel baskets in which the Baldwins and Greenings, Russets, and Blue Pearmains were hauled from the sidehill orchard to the bins in the barn where they were heaped until they were sorted.

To farm children, Sam was more than a ladder and basket man. He brought news of friends and relatives from surrounding towns; he knew all the country gossip and scandal that didn't interest children, but seemed to have meaning for Father and Mother. Many times Sam arrived late in the afternoon and put up his handsome, chunky team of bay geldings in the barn. In the evening Sam told stories and jokes, reminisced with Father and played his harmonica before young fry were sent to bed. And in the morning, after business was transacted and Mother was presented a dainty, sweet-fern basket, Sam never failed. He reached under the seat and brought out a striped, red and green bag of hard candies for each of the expectant young folks. "So long," he said, and started up the road. "So long, see you next year."

The Golden Tinge

There comes a time in August when the mellow hue of gold is woven into the countryside. It is not the deep gold of early autumn; it is not a color that overpowers the greens of lush meadows. But the gold of autumn is on the way, and the fringes of soft color blend into the landscape. Along country roadsides and upland fields the goldenrod begins to bloom. You see the upright plants with nodding heads along pasture lanes and fences, outlining the land in a thin gold frame.

Stand above a corn field on a sun-bright day and wait for a vagrant breeze. Clouds of golden pollen grains lift from the tassels and sail away. Corn leaves have a golden-green color that foretells the day when the leaves will be thin gold and kernels full in the ear. There is gold in the evergreens' needles when you see them in the slanting rays at dawn or sunset; there is gold in fields of ripening oats and barley and wheat. Gold is the sign of maturity; gold is the augury of harvest.

The air is alive with bright butterflies, and the stately Monarch rides passing breezes on fluttering wings of brown and tan, orange, black, and gray. You can always identify the Monarch by the double circle of white dots on the black edges of all four wings. The sharply etched black veins in the shaded colorings of orange and tan look like the pastel beauty of stained glass windows.

Soon these butterflies will congregate in flocks and move southward for the winter. Next season they will come back, lay their eggs and nature's cycle will be re-enacted. You know it is the heart of summer when the Monarchs are dancing in the sun.

Goldfinches add a splash of color to the August landscape. The goldfinch is a good example for man. It takes life as it comes; it finds joy in each day of living; and yet before the summer has gone, it has performed its duty. These happy-go-lucky birds are often called wild canaries, yellow birds, or thistle birds because they use the down of thistles for nest lining. Many times the nests are not built until late July or early August. The four or five small eggs are a pale blue-gray.

The thistle bird gets along with its peers, and often one sees sizable flocks swooping over the fields and meadows in undulating flight. At the crest of the wavelike flight, their sweet, canary-like notes may tumble out and sow the summer air with pleasant music. One of August's most appealing pictures is a flock of goldfinches in breeding plumage feeding on a green lawn. The pure lemon-gold and glossy black of the little birds against an expanse of green is a scene to remember.

In late August, the birds begin to gather in large flocks. There are no more bubbling cascades of music. Now the thistle birds give their familiar plaintive cheeps as they fly from one feeding spot to another. Soon the glowing gold and gleaming black of the males will fade to olive green. Soon most will start their southward journey, although some will remain in northern areas through the winter. The goldfinch does not seem to bother about trivial details. Perhaps the goldfinch knows that too much attention to small matters detracts from the main purpose of living.

August Flowers

Wild asters string necklaces along the roadsides. They fill field corners with soft beauty and mingle with ferns along pasture lanes. You see them high on hills where dirt roads wander along the uplands and then dip down to creek-traversed lowlands. Asters flourish on pasture slopes and grow along the edges of woodlots. Their brilliant purple is the first hint of the bright autumn colors to come.

There are some 250 species of asters and many varieties within each species. The composite family is one of the largest in the botanical kingdom—a family that includes goldenrod, dandelions and sunflowers. The aster clan is widely distributed over the United States, and if a man desired he could devote a lifetime's study to them and still have unanswered questions.

The New England aster is one of the prominent members. Named for the land of the Pilgrim Fathers, it is at home east of the Mississippi. Possibly it is the showiest aster of all; sometimes it grows six feet tall and flowers are frequently a full inch across. It often has from forty to fifty rays around its glowing yellow center.

Study a patch of the blossoms in a breeze, and watch the purple hues change from dark to light and back again as the wind ruffles the petals. The flaming red and gold of the maples and the wine and bronze of the oaks will soon be spectacular. The asters are advance scouts and their purple flowers foretell autumn's glory.

The rich lilac-purple beauty of the milkweed joins the eighth-month countryside display of goldenrod, hardhack, joe-pye weed and asters. We take the common milkweed for granted, but it is an unusual plant. The milkweed family, some 2000 species in about 220 genera, is widely spread although most species are in the warmer temperate and tropical areas. The name "milkweed" was given long ago because of the milky-colored, sticky juice in the stems and leaves. American Indians ate the young shoots and squaws used the fluffy down for household purposes. When the dried seed pods break open, the winged seeds ride away on the breeze and are frequently carried long distances. Seed pods will not mature and open until cool weather settles in, but now the loveliness of milkweed blossoms adds color to the pre-autumn scene.

These hot summer days cattails stand like chocolate-headed exclamation points above the lush greenness of the sloughs, swales and swamps. Their long, slender leaves are often taller than the brown blossom stalks. This perennial herb has been tagged with many aliases: cat-o'-nine-tails, marsh beetle, marsh pestle, cattail flag, water toch and candlewick. *Typha latiofolia*, its scientific name, tells two facts about the cattail. Typha means a bog, and latifolia means broad-leaved.

The Indians used cattail roots in the spring for food. In late summer the roots store large quantities of starch. Records tell us that Virginia settlers boiled the blossoms and made a soup. Colonists used the strong stems for candles, putting a wick through the hollow stem; and many a man of mature years can recall the torchlight political parades at the turn of the century when he dipped a cattail head in coal oil for a torch.

If you belong to the group which applauds the loud and brassy, the showy and spectacular, the modest pasture rose of New England hillsides will not appeal. In this superlative-prone era, the unpretentious loveliness of the common pasture rose is a refreshing antidote to the garishness of neon signs and blatant billboards.

The pasture rose is the ancestor of the tremendous variety of cultivated roses. Somewhere I once read that the magnificent rose gardens of America with their carefully tended beds and displays of many colors are the finest expression of gardening in the New World. But the next time you see a magnificent display in a rose garden or a gorgeous bouquet of long-stemmed beauties in a florist's window, remember that the beautiful blossoms trace back to the unassuming loveliness of the pasture rose.

On a sun-drenched slope where granite rocks and gray birches provide accent points, you may find a sizable area covered with the trailing vines, the small, deep-green leaves, the thorn-covered stems, and the glowing pink-red flowers of the pasture rose. It is a beautiful flower, small but perfectly proportioned. Its five petals are red, streaked with gray-green, with the deepest color near the outside. In the center there is a prominent circle of short-stemmed stamens with little shoe-box anthers of golden pollen. In late summer the deep-red hips, or fruits, gleam like jewels in the bright sunshine.

Botanically, the pasture rose is an interesting plant. Each blossom has only two or perhaps three days of life. If you follow a bed of the ground-trailing flowers from blossom time until autumn, you know that on a cloudy or rainy day, the petals fold inward to protect the yellow stamens and the heart-clump of greenish stigmas. Each evening as the sun sinks behind the mountain rim, the blossoms close; in early dawn as the sun's rays light the countryside the petals open again.

I have read that in olden days, the red hips were used as food. In old journals one can find reference to them. "Children with great delight eat the berries thereof when they are ripe, and make chaines and other pretty geegaws of the fruit; cookes and gentlewomen make tarts and such like dishes for pleasure." The hips are handsome fruits and very appealing, but I have found their puckery tartness unpleasant to the taste. It is conjecture, of course, but I wonder if it was part of nature's plan to make the fruit so attractive that birds would take them and drop the seeds in other places, thus guaranteeing the spread of the species.

Another botanically interesting fact is the pasture rose's pointed, downward-slanted thorns or prickles. These prickles effectively discourage cattle from eating the branches and keep field mice from climbing along the stems to the ripe fruits. I have watched insects come to the wild rose for its pollen. Small insects light on the petals and crawl about, but a bumblebee lights directly on the collar of stamens. The petals are so fragile that a heavy bumblebee cannot find secure footing.

August brings a gay variety of old-fashioned garden flowers into bloom. It is not that I am opposed to new things because they are new; plant scientists are constantly creating miracles with juggled chromosomes. But some of the exotic new creations do not have the homey appeal of flowers that are carefully tended in the bed beneath the kitchen windows. The tall, stately hollyhock is perhaps the most colorful of all and provides a bright background for the zinnias, calendulas, and phlox. The name hollyhock comes from two old Anglo-Saxon words: *holi*, because the plants were originally brought to England by the Crusaders, and *hoc*, a word that means mallow. Linnaeus, the Swedish botanist, gave it the pleasant botanical name, *Althaea rosea*. In his time, the 1700's, plants were considered important for their medicinal value, and *Althaea rosea* derives from a Greek word meaning "to cure."

So far as research reveals, there is no hollyhock native to the

New World. Early settlers brought seeds from England. When pioneers crossed the mountains and flatboated down the rivers to the West, when prairie schooners lumbered across the plains, wives and mothers carried hollyhock seeds to add color to their new gardens far from the Atlantic seaboard. Hollyhocks are flowers that mean home. They represent stability and tradition, and the fact that they are old-fashioned flowers means something to those who cherish a link with the past.

Bee Lining

On a sunny, late summer day when the bees were working the wild asters or goldenrod, it was both interesting and enjoyable sport to line bees. There was always the possibility that you could line the wild bees to their home in a tree and get a generous supply of honey. Wild bees are those that have left the colonies and made a new home. Most persons think that when a colony swarms, it is a new queen that comes forth with perhaps half the bees, but it is the old queen that leaves with many followers. The swarm commonly concentrates on the limb of a nearby tree and waits for scout bees to return and report on a new location.

What happens is this. As a colony in a hive increases in numbers during the spring flow of nectar, several queen cells are formed on the frames. These future queens are fed a special food, and the first young queen that hatches goes around and stings the unhatched new queens to death. This leaves two queens in one realm—the older, mated queen and the newly-hatched virgin queen. Nature has developed the instincts that now come into play. The old queen leaves with her retinue; the virgin queen goes out for her mating flight and returns to the hive. Then the newly-mated queen carries on in the old hive, laying hundreds of eggs a day in a good season. Thus, if the beekeeper cuts the queen cells from the supers, the old queen does not leave. The colony may build up to 50,000 or more bees, largely workers. The only life purpose of the drones is to mate with a young queen. In the fall, the workers drive the drones out and they die. New drones are raised each spring.

Perhaps you have seen hives with many "supers," or boxes

for honey storage. If swarming is prevented, a strong colony may make a hundred pounds of honey. But swarms escape in the best-run apiaries, and the bees make homes in hollow trees. It is these wild bees that offer good sport and fun in the late summer. Naturally, one waits as late as possible to get the most honey.

A bee box is a small container in two parts with a sliding glass cover. You put a little chunk of honey in one of the parts, and then find a honeybee on a flower and brush it into the box. In a minute or so, the bee finds the honey and loads up. You open the cover and the bee circles upward and heads for its home.

Now comes one of nature's inscrutable mysteries. How does that first bee tell its fellow workers it has found a source of honey? If all goes well, in a few minutes the original bee returns with a few of its friends. They go into the box and load up. You close the glass top and with the bees in the box, walk as far as you consider wise in the direction in which the first bee flew. Then you let the bees out again and repeat the process. Sometimes you have to walk a considerable distance if you are on an open hillside or in a wide meadow. When there are trees about, you only have to go a short distance.

Sometimes it took all day to follow the wild bees to their tree; sometimes you did not find it at all. But if you were fortunate, the trips of the bees took progressively less time. When you finally located the bee tree, the real excitement began. You got permission from the landowner to cut the tree, and it was the custom in our region also to give the owner some of the honey.

If you wished to play it safe, you waited until a night of killing frost and went to the tree in the cold early morning. Even so, chopping the tree, or sawing it, was likely to start up the bees. When the tree crashed, you dashed in with a pail of smoldering bark and stuffed it into the hole. It was fun to line the bees; it was exciting to fell the tree. And a milkpail of good honey was worth a few stings.

Aerial Circus

Many a farmer planning to mow a few acres of thick, second-growth clover or alfalfa first takes a minute to watch the barn swallows. If they are flying high it means good weather; for in warm weather and low humidity, insects are carried hundreds of feet into the air with upward air currents. Then the swallows do their hunting high, circling and swooping, diving and climbing, harvesting a mouthful to take back to hungry young in mud-plastered nests against barn rafters. If swallows are flying low, however, it means the air is cooler, and perhaps a rain is on the way.

The male swallow is a handsome fellow with glowing red-brown forehead and throat. The deeply forked tail is a distinctive feature. With the possible exception of the chimney swift, no small bird is more graceful in flight. Barn swallows have excellent dispositions and a dozen or more pairs frequently build their nests in the same barn. If a wandering cat or marauding weasel appears, all the swallows join in attacking the enemy.

Originally these friendly birds nested in hollow trees, in caves and beneath hillside ledges. But when white men built barns and bridges, icehouses and woodsheds, they quickly adopted buildings for nesting locations. The mud nests are strengthened with grasses and straw, and because the nests are under cover, they rarely fall. Most pairs raise two broods a year from the brown-and-lilac spotted eggs. As summer wears on, the swallows finish up housekeeping for the year, and long lines of the graceful birds sit on telephone wires above country roads getting organized for their trip to Mexico and points south.

Long before man learned to fly, chimney swifts were sweeping the evening skies for insects. It is interesting that this member of the family *Micropodidae* so wholeheartedly adopted man's high brick chimneys for its summer home. They feed only on the wing and in forty years of bird study, I have never seen a swift light on the ground. Only five inches in length, they have a wing spread of twelve to thirteen inches and strong spikes in their tails to brace themselves against the chimney wall. Their nests are crude half-saucers of twigs, glued by "saliva" to the vertical chimney wall. The four or five eggs are pure white; and many a housewife has found a nest, broken eggs, or several young birds in the living-room fireplace.

When day is almost done and gray-purple shadows are

stretching from posts and silos, the swifts stage their evening aerial circus. They swoop and circle, climb and dive. They are unbelievably fast. They climb high in the air and then suddenly, like a squadron of airplanes, head earthward and pull up at the last moment.

As day retreats it is relaxing to sit on a screened farm porch and watch swifts dash through the air. When the katydids begin to call and night's curtain is almost lowered, the swifts settle in the chimney for the night with loud staccato twitterings. In the small hours when a man wakens, he can hear the birds talk behind the wall. Housewives may not be partial to the swifts, but somehow it is part of summer to listen to their nightly discussion in the chimney.

Teaching Pullets to Roost

Adult citizens of our social order may be arbitrarily divided into two main groups: those who like hens and those who do not. I am not arguing that hens have a high I.Q.; anyone who has tried to drive a hen in a reasonable facsimile of a straight line appreciates that hens, like some people, do not wish to attain a goal by traveling a straight path.

But there are those who enjoy the companionship of the egg producers. It is pleasantly relaxing for a man to talk to his hens and listen to their comments. A flock of pullets in late summer, just redding up to lay, is a pretty picture. Hens are excellent weather prophets; if they stand around, jawing and arguing instead of attending to scratching for worms and bugs, one can be reasonably certain of a storm within thirty-six hours.

There is one task that admittedly tries a man's patience and sandpapers his nerves. Teaching pullets to roost on hot, sticky evenings is a monotonous and long-drawn-out process. At heavy dusk a man goes to the coop, picks up the pullets from the floor and sets them on the roost. Night after night, a man leaves his comfortable rocking chair and repeats the process. Approximately seventy-five percent of the young ladies learn the lesson reasonably quickly; another twenty percent absorb the idea within a fortnight. But five percent are stubborn and apparently completely allergic to education. I probably should not be unduly discouraged or alarmed. In observing my fellow human beings, it appears that somewhat more than five percent of them have not managed to learn life's lessons.

Hammocks

In the pleasant days of yesteryear when covered bridges were an essential part of the landscape and owning a fringe-topped surrey was a mark of distinction, a man liked to stretch out comfortably in an old-fashioned woven hammock. I remember that the Mexican woven hammock made of sisal twine was only 80 cents; for 85 cents there was a cotton-weave hammock with pillow and spreader. If you wanted to step up to $1.20, there was a good outfit made of a close, fancy canvas weave with a highly-colored spreader and pillow. But nothing could touch the Damask Pattern Tufted Pillow Hammock. The catalog's description was good: "Our largest sized, tufted pillow hammock. Made in glowing, gorgeous, full, fancy colors with strong spreader and detachable, tufted pillow with extra wood bar as shown in the illustration. Full, deep, beautiful colored valance at sides. Size of bed 40 by 80 inches. We consider this the best bargain ever offered in hammocks. Weight, 10 pounds. Our special price $2.55."

Of course, if finances were strained, an up-and-coming farmer could make himself a barrel-stave hammock. If this was well padded with old patchwork quilts and perhaps a horse blanket or two, it was very comfortable. In fact, some countrymen preferred the firmness of the barrel staves to the softness of the woven textile affair.

We need a hammock renaissance in this nation. Life is speeded to an unnatural tempo. We have made tremendous material strides in one generation, but in our getting and spending we have lost much that we need for the enjoyment of living. A hammock wouldn't solve all our problems, but it would be a step in the right direction.

August Evening

When the katydids begin their chanting on a humid August evening, the countryman may be forgiven a half sigh, for he knows now that summer is gliding downhill toward autumn. As the katydids begin to fiddle he says to himself, "Six more weeks until frost."

Contrary to what many think, the katydids do not sing, but chant. These insects which resemble large-winged grasshoppers spend their time on bushes and trees and eat leaves. Most katydids are a rich green color, with finely-veined sheaths protecting the wings which are used in gliding, rather than flying. Eggs are laid in the soft bark of twigs and small branches. The adults die when cold weather arrives, and the species is carried on when the eggs hatch the following spring. In late fall when grasshoppers and crickets become silent, the katydids, protected by leaves, often continue to chant until a black, killing frost.

After an honest day's work in the fields, a man is glad to sit on the farmhouse porch and rock slowly back and forth while a waxing, yellow-orange August moon climbs into the sky and starts slicing a path among the stars. It is warm and humid and you can feel the heavy moistness in the air. While the katydids play their rasping fiddle notes, moths flutter against the porch screening, and in the back pasture a fox barks at the night.

Far out in the vast astral reaches of our universe, the Perseids, flaming spears of the gods, write red exclamation points against the blue-blackness of the sky. None has ever been known to reach our earth. But as they burn out in the upper strata, a man begins to think of the universe stretching hundreds of millions of miles from where he sits.

As shadows deepen, fragrances intensify. If a man has been hoeing in the late afternoon, the pungent aroma of fresh-stirred soil is heady and satisfying. There's a musky fragrance from the tomatoes and a pleasantly spicy aroma from the cucumber bed. Stand beside the corn patch as darkness deepens and moist air settles, and you will get a peculiar, slightly acid smell. There are those who disagree, but some men honestly believe they can hear corn grow. As your ears become accustomed to small sounds and sift out the chants of crickets and the little noises that scratch against the curtain of darkness, you may possibly hear a faint, hollow, rustling sound—a sound which you cannot hear any other season of the year. You cannot say for certain that it is the stretching upward of the corn leaves, but it is satisfying to think so.

The hermit thrush adds its lovely music to the sounds of an August night. Until you have listened to the bird from no more than twenty or thirty feet you have little conception of the power, brilliancy, and melodiousness of its song. On a still evening the song may carry a quarter-mile. Yet the depth and range of the silvery tones, and the lighter runs and trills, cannot be heard unless you are reasonably close.

The hermit is our most exquisite vocalist and the hardiest of its group. It comes northward in the spring three or four weeks ahead of other thrushes and it waits in autumn until other thrushes have left before starting its journey southward. On a peaceful August evening his song is a fitting benediction.

SEPTEMBER

ONE PERFECT SEPTEMBER DAY CAN COMPENSATE FOR A spell of bad weather, although what the urbanite may label "bad" is frequently what the farmer needs for his land. The day is warm but not uncomfortably so; humidity is low and there is a gentle hint of a cool-edged breeze from the west. Daylight comes slowly as blackness bleaches to a gray-purple hue. Hilltops across the valley catch the first shafts of light. As the sun pulls itself above the horizon, patches of white-gray mist hover over the meadows and scattered wisps of fog on the higher hillsides begin to move upward.

High noon on a sunny September day is one of the year's most pleasant times. Gone is the sticky humidity that ruled while the Dog Star cruised across the daytime August sky; this is a season when the husbandman can watch the final maturing of his crops and make ready for the harvest. Purple and maroon are the royal hues of autumn; tall spikes of ironweed fringe the sloughs, and streaks of maroon are spreading in the leaves of swamp maples.

Flocks of goldfinches swoop and swirl in leisurely fashion over the fields; crickets fiddle unhurriedly in the pleasant warmth. You can smell the warmed soil and the fragrance of ripening apples heavy on the bough. The countryside is coming to the end of another season; nature's schedule is on time.

If you lift your eyes these September days, you notice that the hills are getting ready for fall. Early in the ninth month, you begin to see familiar signs. Red leaves start to show bright pennants against a green background. Sumac clumps on ledged hillsides are fiery blotches of color above amber grasses. On sloping mountain shoulders and granite-topped ridges, white birches, spruces and hemlocks are outlined against a blue, cloud-patched sky.

There is a brief, poignant period of beauty just before the flaming colors of autumn spread over hills and valleys. In this period of readiness, the slanting rays of the sun pick out the scattered colored branches and sharply limn the contours of the uplands. The softness of September air, the cool moistness at dawn and the hint of frost at sundown are reminders that we are sliding downhill from summer now. The seasons of growth and maturing have passed.

The Simple and Straightforward

Joe-pye weed stands tall these late-summer days and its strong stalk holds a cluster of red-purple flowers above brown grasses and weeds. Joe-pye thrives in moist soil and enjoys either open land or semi-shadowed woodland if it can keep its roots moist. Joe-pye weed isn't a fragile bloom that appeals to the tender sentiments. Named for an Indian herb doctor who lived in the Pilgrim days, it is an extrovertish flower that often holds its head six feet or more above ground.

Whenever you go near moist soil in September you are likely to see these tall plants with their eye-arresting blossoms in meadows, along creeks, and around edges of swamps. From New Brunswick to Manitoba and south to the Rio Grande, joe-pye lifts royal purple pennants that foretell autumn.

I do not know whether Joe Pye actually cured the typhus with a concoction made from the plant. Legend says that another name for joe-pye was "spotted boneset" because with his medicine, the herb doctor could stop the shaking of ague-plagued bodies. In some regions the plant is called trumpetweed or thoroughwort. But we prefer to think of this upstanding plant with flamboyant blossom clusters as plain joe–pye weed. That's a good, straightforward label. Of course if you insist on scientific nomenclature, you can speak of *Eupatorium maculatum*. That is technically correct, but somehow joe–pye and technology don't go together. Joe–pye weed is an uninhibited, straight-from-the-shoulder type. And the name fits well.

Come this time of year, Father began to watch the six or eight acres where we cut the rowen. This area of good loam soil usually produced two generous cuttings of tall hay, and in the fall, the rowen was perhaps eight to ten inches high. I have never seen an analysis of autumn rowen versus timothy and clover harvested in June, but I remember that Father and other farmers agreed there were superior feeding qualities in this end-of-the-season crop. I remember we dried it carefully and stored the loads in a special section of the west scaffold.

I thought of this the other day as I cut my own rowen crop. I have a spot where I raise grass just for mulching. This is the fourth crop I have taken from it this year. My wife laughs at me because a good percentage of the grass is witch grass, but in case you are interested, witch grass makes excellent mulching material. Come to think of it, it is the only use I have for it, but farmers have told me that if witch grass is cut before it gets too mature, it makes good hay for cows.

The rowen grass is different. This isn't typical hay; it is short, limp grass which makes excellent material to put between strawberries grown in the hill system. It is good under Scarlet Beauty shell beans to keep the big pods off the soil. I like to scatter it around tomatoes which are allowed to grow nature's way. I use it to cover the wire on the ground that is part of my woodchuck fence.

Rowen time brings back memories of the long ago. If Father mowed the rowen on a Thursday, with good weather conditions it would be cured by Saturday. As soon as the moisture was off, Old Jerry and I raked it up and put it into scraggly cocks with the horse-drawn hayrake. In the afternoon, Father and I would bring it up to the barn, where he pitched off and I mowed away. Rowen time is a good time of year. I enjoy the fragrance of the spicy-sweet grass. Perhaps I like rowen time because from

(185)

mid-September to mid-October is my favorite four-week period of year. Rowen is the last crop of the hayfield, and perhaps there is a feeling in a man that is satisfied as crops are harvested.

Stacking Beans

After a black frost, Father was likely to say at Saturday breakfast on a sunny, crisp morning, "Son, better stack the beans today." A generation ago, farmers were proud of their red kidneys, yellow eyes, and northern pea beans. A countryman wanted baked beans for Saturday supper and Sunday breakfast, baked with his home-raised, lean salt pork and sweetened with his own maple syrup.

Stacking beans wasn't particularly hard work, but it was monotonous. Each stack had a pole with stubby branches to hold the beans in place. After a lad cut the poles and trimmed the branches to about a foot in length, he set the poles in holes made with a crowbar. Around each pole he placed old boards to protect the bottom layer of beans. Handful by handful, the frost-brittle, leathery plants with dried pods were pulled. Soil was knocked off against an overalled leg; the plants were jammed, roots first, among the pole's stubs. Each stack was built with the roots higher than the leaves and pods to shed rain. Hour by hour a boy worked along. Hour by hour, the stacks increased in number and when day was done he could feel satisfaction in having done the job. After a few weeks in the fall air, the stacks were hauled to the barn to wait for flailing when work was not so pressing.

Picklin' Time

There is a nostril-tickling, spicy, pungent fragrance these days in farm kitchens. It spreads through the summer kitchen and drifts into the woodshed where a man is stacking tiers of wood against the cold ahead. It is picklin' time on the farm and the kettles of simmering pickles, ketchup, chutney, and chili sauce mean flavorful accompaniments for meat and baked beans in the months ahead.

I have read that Caesar's army demanded pickles on its war expeditions. George Washington wrote in appreciation of pickles. Thomas Jefferson said, "On a hot day, I know of nothing more comforting than a fine, spiced pickle." In any case, housewives have been making pickles for years. In many families there are cherished recipes handed down for generations. Some citizens like their pickles sweet and some like them sour. The finishing process is a matter of flavoring with sugar, salt, vinegar, and spices, but the caliber of the product depends upon the recipe used. I like my pickles, chutney, and chili sauce on the sweet side, but I will settle most of the time for sweet-tart bread-and-butter pickles. I appreciate, however, that under our form of government every member of a family is entitled to his own taste. Boughten pickles are good and their sale is on the increase, but I still like the special fragrance that comes from the pickling kettles.

Debating, Sermonizing and Milking

It was through Mr. Parker, the tobacco-chewing, temporary teacher, that I first began debating. The *Peterborough Transcript*, our local weekly paper, reported in the fall of 1914, "A Debating Club was formed in the eighth grade of the Hancock School and Haydn Pearson was elected president."

The Debating Club got off to a good start. We learned the rules; we learned to search for the strongest arguments. Mr. Parker insisted that we get all the arguments on both sides of a question so that in the rebuttal period we would have available ammunition. One of his favorite projects was to have a team debate one side of a question on a Friday afternoon, and then take the opposite side the next Friday.

The Friday afternoon school program drew quite a few listeners. Father had been on the debating team at Bates College, and he coached me; he taught me to hit two or three main arguments instead of listing too many reasons. Later, when I was at the University of New Hampshire and on the debating team, I kept Father's advice in mind. Each Friday afternoon, Mr. Parker asked three visitors to be judges and if Father were there, he was asked. Father was scrupulously fair and when my side lost, or the other for that matter, he would talk to us a few minutes and point out why one side had not gotten across its points.

So I became a debater. Mother and my sisters did not particularly like the idea of my orating in the house. Father sometimes practiced his sermons in the living room with the door shut, but he never really let out. I don't know how it began, but soon I was practicing my debating arguments while I was milking. Father used the same time to practice his sermon. In that period we had about a dozen milking cows in the tie-up. Father began milking at one end; I started at the other. Let's say the topic for the next debate was: "Resolved, country life is more moral than city life." I had my two or three reasons, and as the first arrows of milk pinged musically into the pail and the head of white froth began to rise, I warmed to my subject.

Meanwhile, Father was getting steamed up. In his sermons he always started in a conversational tone, and then as he went along his voice began to rise. In his prime Father had a wonderful speaking voice, powerful, far-carrying, and resonant. He had been trained in old-fashioned oratory and he knew how to pull out the stops. "Good practice for the throat," he said.

I tried to copy Father in my speaking. I learned to pause. I discovered that a question often got a point across. I would speak slowly for a minute in a low tone; then I would suddenly shout and try to drive home a point. So we milked, debated, and sermonized. The cows? They were friendly, placid creatures and after one or two sessions, I am sure they assumed it was perfectly natural for a man and a boy to shout or whisper as they milked.

One late afternoon we were milking, and both of us were in good form. We were shouting and sermonizing and having a good time. Unknown to us neighbor John Adams came into the barn. Father was going all out, exhorting the faithful to be more so and giving the Devil about all it deserved. Mr. Adams came along the walk behind the cows with a big smile on his face. "Well, Elder," he said, "I've heard you give us a good going-over from the pulpit many times, and I guess we all need it. But this is the first time I ever knew that you had to preach to cows."

Old Iron Kettles

Do you remember the old, heavy iron kettles that were part of the farmstead equipment half a century and more ago? I can still see the big kettle that Mother used to make stews, soups, and chowders. It held a good six quarts and sat in the hole of one of the front rimmers of the wood-burning stove. It had four stubby legs so it could be placed on a level surface; and around the bottom was a half-inch flange so that it fitted snugly into the cover hole and the flame could hit it directly.

Under the brick arch in the summer kitchen, there was an iron kettle that probably held twenty-five gallons. This was used for boiling clothes before we had the more familiar tin boilers. Once or twice Father and I used this kettle to boil down sap, but Mother objected to the dense clouds of steam. Thereafter we used the hanging kettle in the backyard between the plum trees. We used to speculate how long this kettle had been used. Long before we came to the farm, two big posts, trunks of trees with Y crotches, had been set up. The posts were about twelve inches in diameter, and the crotches were about six feet from the ground; a solid peeled pole stretched between the crotches. Then another strong limb or small tree trunk with a big hook angle of a branch hung from this crossbar. A notch had been cut into the lower end, and from this notch hung the kettle, so that it was a foot or a bit more from the ground.

The fireplace here in our living room, the original kitchen plus the borning room, will take a five-foot log without crowding. Sometimes on a cold and windy night as the zero temperature pulls clapboards from nails, I look at that big fireplace with its crane and hook. Here, long ago, a farm wife prepared the meals. A soot-crusted kettle hung from the crane; perhaps an iron Dutch oven sat on the hearth facing the heat. The brick oven to the left is where the bread and cakes, Indian puddings and suet puddings were baked.

Perhaps you remember the iron teakettles with the V-shaped opening of the snout and the wooden handle fashioned around the bale. There is an old-timer that I have not seen since boyhood; I think it was called an iron bake oven. It was about ten inches in diameter and had a heavy, tight-fitting cover. The kettle could be set into the fireplace coals for roasting meats. Scotch bowls were shallow iron kettles without covers, but with a flange around the bottom so they could be set into a stove cover opening.

The only iron utensil we use now is the old spider. But once again I'd like to come in from evening chores on the old farm, and see Mother stirring something in that old, black, soot-bottomed iron kettle, and whiff the fragrance that filled the lamplighted kitchen.

Line Storm

Today men probably think very little of my grandfather's claim that equinoxes bring line storms. Meteorologists say that a storm at the time of the equinox is simply a coincidence. When specific conditions develop in the atmosphere we have a storm, and the fact that days and nights are approximately equal has no relationship to the weather.

So say the experts. But countrymen who live with the weather look for and expect a line storm along in September. Naturally, a man does not insist that the line storm will come precisely on the date of the equinox. But one of these days the wind will swing around and there will be a cool, cutting edge, and the white cumulus clouds will change to cirrus.

You can feel a line storm in the air and hear it as the wind freshens. At dusk jays scream as they flash above the orchard. By morning the cloud veil will have thickened and darkened, and nimbus clouds will hang low. Hour by hour the wind will develop power, the rawness in the air will increase, and then the rain will begin. It may not be scientifically proven but it always seems to happen, just as Grandfather said it would.

Nature's Own

You know that summer is heading southward when the stag-horn sumac's spear-pointed leaves change from green to flaming red. Sometimes it takes days for the transformation; in some years the change seems to come overnight. Driving his cows along the road to the pasture, the countryman suddenly notices that the sumacs are fire-red, and he knows that a change of season is due.

The staghorn was growing in the Virginia region some eighteen or twenty million years before the Ice Age, and when the era of ice ended, the shrub traveled northward. Now it is a familiar part of the New England landscape. The tall shrub or small tree grows from a few feet to thirty or forty feet high. The staghorn received its picturesque name because the velvety-haired, irregular branches resemble the horns of a stag. The wood is light, brittle, and coarse, but has a beautiful grain. It is of little commercial value, although farmers once used its hollowed stems for spiles in maple sugar season.

Now the staghorn holds its bright leaves along roadsides, in the corners of fields, and along the edges of woodlands where nature is taking back land that man once claimed for his use. The conical, white-green, flower clusters of June have changed to wine-red. The red leaves and flower clusters shine through September days.

The humble gray is a member of the widespread birch family. Untold millions of years ago in what is now the ice-covered Arctic region, birches developed unusual elasticity in their cells. Scientists tell us that while the tundra regions were whipped by pressing winds, the birches probably came into being. As aeons of time passed, continents became fixed, mountain ranges were heaved into position, and the polar region cooled to a land of perpetual ice and snow. We do not know just how and when the birches migrated southward. Farmers have given the gray birch several names: poplar birch, poverty birch, old field birch and small white birch. This small tree has leaves that are a thin, glossy green, triangular, and sharp-toothed with a fine-notched edge.

The gray does not pretend to compete with the beautiful white birch, the spectacular red, the dignified black, or the handsome yellow. The everyday gray fills the field corners of neglected mowings; it finds a place among country roads and makes its home on pasture hillsides. The other members of the family like the rich soil of woodlands, meadows, and river valleys; the gray strikes down its roots in sandy soil and in neglected places.

Three centuries ago there were vast stands of handsome, tall sycamores along the valleys of the Mississippi and Ohio rivers. There were sizable groves in the rich, moist lowlands of the Northeast, in the valleys of the Midwest and in the meadows at the foothills of the Alleghanies. In fertile, damp soil, the spectacular sycamore often reaches a height of seventy-five to one hundred feet; in girth it is the largest deciduous tree in our country.

The sycamore is often called the buttonwood because its fruit develops into brown, round balls that hang from long, wiry stems. The ball surface is rough with nutlets which break off during the winter and the seeds are carried long distances by the wind. The most distinctive feature of this interesting tree is its large cream-white blotches. The bark of most species of trees furrows and cracks as the trunk expands; but the sycamore's bark is peculiarly inelastic, and huge flakes of the outer brown bark periodically fall off, exposing an arresting, eye-catching pattern of light-colored under-surface patches.

A century and more ago the sycamore served many needs on farms, for the wood is heavy, coarse-grained, strong and hard. It was used for homemade furniture and farm implements. Now the extensive forests of the handsome sycamores are gone. But here and there in river valleys, in mountain meadows and beside woodland streams, you can still see these handsome trees, lifting their branches high to wind and rain and sun.

Picking Apples

I wish all men could take a few days off in early autumn to pick apples. I am an apple fan, and that is perhaps why I do not condemn Adam too severely. We should remember that Eve tempted him with an apple, and if she had one of the better varieties, it is not at all surprising that Adam fell. On a sunny fall day, picking apples is one of the best tasks in the list of annual farm jobs. There is more to apple picking than filling a basket and climbing up and down a ladder. If you are not pressed for time, you can pause for a spell and savor the goodness of the season. There is a heady, spicy fragrance in the air; purple haze shimmers on the hillsides across the valley, and in the distance the mountains are blue-green against the horizon. The valley river resembles a twisted silver thread; and overhead, white clouds graze in shaggy flocks across the upstairs meadow.

Picking apples has its fringe benefits, too; namely, cider. Half a century and more ago many farms had small hand-operated cider presses, and good farmers often put down a few barrels of juice to sell months later as vinegar. We wish all city boys could know the satisfaction of kneeling beside a half-tub of the golden-amber juice, pressed through layers of pomace and burlap. The old cider mill at the foot of the hill was a popular spot. The man who made the cider, either for cash or on shares, was tolerant of twelve-year-olds who came in with long oat straws. The capacity of a twelve-year-old's stomach is the eighth wonder of the world, and the old miller never ceased to marvel at the amount a lad could consume.

What do I remember best about apples? Unless you have made apple butter in a large quantity, you won't fully sympathize or understand what I mean when I say making apple butter was a major event. The apples were peeled on the apple parer attached to a leaf of the old cherry table in the kitchen. Sisters threw long peelings over their shoulders to see if they could find the initials of the Prince Charming that was to come their way. The apples were cored and quartered.

My place of operation was in the backyard where the big kettle hung. Early in the morning I started the fire and boiled down the sweet cider to the consistency that Mother wanted. Then the apples went in and the day's long, wearisome, and monotonous job began. The apples had to be stirred from the time they went in until that wonderful moment when Mother finally decided it was time to stop. I'll never forget that old peeled stick with the crook at the end. All day long the stirring went on—round and round and round.

In the late afternoon, Mother kept her eye on the dark-looking mass. I don't remember all that she put in, but there were cloves, cinnamon, allspice, a little sugar, and I think some lemon juice. Day was ended by the time the butter was finished. Father came around to see how things were going. We all had small amounts to taste. "What do you think, Frank?" Mother would ask. Father tasted slowly and judiciously. "Just right, Rosie," he would say, and I knew the long process was over.

The Fiddlers

Have you ever heard anyone say that you can tell the temperature by a cricket's chirps? Crickets are acknowledged insect thermometers, but the reading can be a complicated process. The common black field cricket is the one that gets into the house, and if your thermometer is not working and you wish to know the temperature count the chirps for fourteen seconds and then add forty. If, by chance, the cricket doesn't chirp for lengthy periods, count the chirps for seven seconds, double the number, and then add eighty. Another fairly common cricket, the snow-tree cricket, is so accurate that some call it the "temperature" cricket. The mathematics here is a trifle different. Count the chirps for fourteen seconds and then add forty-two.

The other evening while I was reading in the study, a cricket began chirping somewhere in the room. I decided to find out just how accurate the little fellow was. But my cricket was having an off night. The temperature in the room was seventy-two; but the cricket consistently missed. He made it sixty one time; a few minutes later I got eighty-four. I don't understand why he alternately chirped slowly and then rapidly. Perhaps he knew I had a thermometer right there anyway.

There are at least 200 species of crickets in the world, and the literature about them goes back to ancient times. Dickens' *Cricket on the Hearth* is part of our heritage. Nathaniel Hawthorne was a cricket fan and wrote, "If moonlight could be heard, it would sound like that." Thoreau spoke of crickets' chirps as "a slumberous breathing." Of course the cricket does not chirp at all. The noise we hear is stridulation. The "chirp" is made by running one wing across the other. The lower side of one wing has a tough material that looks something like a file; the upper surface of the other wing is rough. When the two are rubbed together, a sound is produced which is magnified by the membrane of the wing.

It was a field cricket, *Gryllus assimilis*, that got into my study the other evening. It seems to enjoy human company, or at least the protection of human dwellings. My wife is not so partial to the little fellow as I am. She claims they eat rugs. That may be, but somehow on a September evening when the frost is dropping on the land, I like to hear a cricket chirping in the study. The small black sprite has an optimistic philosophy that I enjoy.

Farm Evenings Long Ago

After a supper of hash, cream of tartar biscuits with raspberry jam, bread-and-butter pickles, juicy, spice-tinged apple pie, and glasses of creamy Guernsey milk, the whole family would spend the evening in the kitchen. Sisters redded up the room and did the dishes while Father and I finished up outside chores by the light of kerosene lanterns.

The big eating table with two chairs on each side and one at each end was covered with a white-and-red-checked cloth. The Lazy Susan with its bottles and shakers sat in the middle; above it was the big, brass-bowled lamp that went up and down on a system of small metal chains. The woodburning stove gleamed and the copper-bottomed teakettle sang a muted melody on the second cover. Sometimes mother mixed up a batch of bread on the old drop-leaf cherry table and set it to rise in a big blue enamel kettle with a piece of linen over the top. Occasionally when I started the fire in the morning, the bread had risen so much that it had overflowed and gray-white rivulets came down the kettle's side.

Father liked to sit by the open oven door with a sizable hand lamp at one end of the eating table to give light. Mother sat in her favorite Boston rocker and worked at the never-quite-caught-up darning and mending. My three sisters and I sat around the table and did our homework before we were supposed to read library books or the *Youth's Companion*. There were times, naturally, when I tucked a small book inside the big, dog-eared geography. But not too often. Not with three sisters who had appointed themselves wardens of a brother who seemed able to get only C's on his report card, while they had no difficulty bringing home monotonous rows of A's.

Sometimes Father would look up from the farm journal, *The Outlook*, or the *World's Work* magazine and say, "Haydn, let's hear that list of state capitals east of the Mississippi." Why was it that I always stumbled over the capital of West Virginia? And why was it that the girls were always so happy to supply the information? If I could guess ahead what Father was likely to ask, I could be ready with the answers. If I felt he would ask me to name the states that bordered Canada, I would learn the list in school and reel them off a mile a minute. But that didn't happen very often.

Those were good times in a boy's life. There was peace and family unity. One had a secure feeling in the days before World War I—a security that has never been achieved since then. Life, we say, was simple in the good old days. National and international problems did not fester in everyone's mind. Now, on these cool evenings of the maturing year, I wish we could recapture those evenings in a lamp-lit farm kitchen.

First Fire

A fireplace is a man's domain, and the lighting of the season's first fire is a pleasant ritual that grows more meaningful as another year of life is written into the records.

Men who enjoy tending a fire are never lonely, for they know the friendly companionship of flames on the hearth. There comes an evening in September when the coolness of approaching autumn brings a definite chill. That is when the countryman lights his first fire of the season, and he prepares carefully for the ritual. Chances are that the ashes have been cleaned out, but that will be remedied soon. All good hearth-keepers know that a heap of ashes is essential for steady warmth. There should be a good-sized backlog of maple, oak, white birch, or ash for firewood. And you need plenty of well-crumpled paper and a generous supply of kindling. Then over the kindling you arrange smaller sticks of split ash, gray birch, or black cherry—quick-catching woods that throw an intense heat.

It isn't the mechanical preparations that count, however, although they are essential. The important point is the spirit behind the first fire. Since man became man, he has tended fires. Our ancestors dreamed and planned, cooked and baked, whittled and wove near leaping flames. We are glad that science has made it possible to warm homes and to cook food by electricity, gas and oil, but we are also happy there are those who appreciate the intangible values of an open fire. For the fire that gives welcome warmth on a cool evening not only means a glow on the hearth. It also means a glow in the heart.

First Frost Tonight

It is always a question up here among the hills and valleys, when the first frost will lay its hand on the cucumbers, melons, squash, and tomatoes. A man goes out nights after supper and spreads old sheets and quilts over some of the vines. The temperature at five A.M., when good country citizens start the day is thirty-three or thirty-four, and you know you have a reprieve for another day. Of course, a hilltop dweller can figure on a longer season at both ends. Light soil on the hilltops dries out earlier in the spring, and some men brag about planting their peas in March. Come fall, these same men hear about the frosts in the lowlands, and pointedly ask how the melons and tomatoes are doing.

Man has figured the precise time when autumn arrives, but there are some years when autumn begins to tap summer on the shoulder early in the month. The countryman can feel the difference at dawn when he goes to the barn for morning chores. The dampness on the woodshed shingles and the cold feel of the pump handle by the barnyard trough tell him that the first frost is near. And then one afternoon a man is certain. The west breeze begins to die and a brooding expectancy settles over the land. The sun sinks behind the mountains and a spectacular sunset flames high toward the zenith and then quickly fades. Shadows push down the eastern slopes and bivouac in the lowlands. Dusk falls quickly now that the turn is here. The cows are impatient to get to the barn and have their grain. Halfway through evening chores, a man lights his lantern and hangs it on the oaken peg in the tie-up.

Coming across the farmyard, with lantern and milk pail on arm, the countryman stops. He sniffs the air; he looks up at the blazing stars. Suddenly, he feels a vagrant wisp of wind—a wind with a cold, sharp edge. This is it. First frost tonight.

OCTOBER

COLORS ARE FLAMING ON THE HILLS. THE VALLEY WOOD-lands are carpets of gold and wine, maroon, bronze and amber. Glory gilds the maple sugar groves. The tall elms by the meadow brook are bouquets of yellow-brown. The limp leaves of wild grape vines pattern the ground and the tangy fragrance of ripe grapes blends with the heady smells of the maturing year.

There are mists on October mornings which look like fluffy gray blankets suspended over the river valleys, swamps, and swales. As dawn light strikes the mountains against the northern horizon, small patches of fog dot the mountainside. As the sun lifts above the pine woods to the east, the fog patches begin to stir and gradually lift and disappear. The colors on the maples and birches are soft and subdued; the maples down in the swale are almost a neutral hue. When the sun climbs into the sky, the color of the maples changes from neutral to a thin yellowish-green, then to amber, and finally they shine like golden candles in the slanting rays.

Ours is truly an autumn-blessed land. There is a change of air in early October. First frosts drift down from the northland and lay chill hands on tomatoes, cucumbers, and squash. Grasses in lowland meadows and on upland fields turn amber. Goldenrod blossoms become gray ghosts, and the rich chocolate of cattails fades to a thinner brown. The first black frost is a turning point of the year. To the countryman, it means real autumn has come to the countryside. After the first killing frost, nature usually relents and sends a fortnight or more of beautiful fall weather. If a man can protect his tomatoes at the beginning of the month, he is likely to pick the red fruit well into October.

There is something about the tenth month that lifts the heart. Mornings are crisp and chill; but at high noon pleasant warmth blesses the land. Purple haze shimmers on the hillsides and on the ridges; a gold platter of sun shines in a deep blue sky. Near the horizon, the blue is lighter and blends into the dark green of the evergreen clothed heights.

Fur is thickening on wild animals; woodchucks are almost ready to start their winter's sleep. Apples are red on the bough and acorns are plump in their filagreed saucers. Most of the migratory birds have left, but some starlit night if you go out to savor the chill edge of a breeze, you may hear the faint calls of the wild geese as they wing their way southward.

Another summer has come and gone. Another winter is ahead. But now for a brief interlude, the season is full of fragrance and rich in coloring. This is autumn, the harvest season.

Autumn Voices

There are some who will recall when many general farms raised a small flock of turkeys each season. Along in October, as soon as a lad got home from school it was his task to let the turkeys out of their pen behind the barn and follow them as they wandered over the fields, into the meadows, or up through the sidehill orchard. Father always put bells on half a dozen of the strutting toms. The bells were small, about two inches in diameter. "Enables the flock to be easily located and makes foxes shy," dogmatically declared the mail-order catalog. Each bell came with a narrow leather strap. It wasn't a bad job at all, following the turkeys as they ranged slowly over the fields and meadows. The tinkling of the small bells was pleasant music on an October day, and perhaps the notes did help keep the foxes away.

There are few sounds more appealing than the faint cries of wild geese in the autumn darkness. High above the earth, the majestic birds are flying in wedge formation, winging their way southward on the high roads of the sky. In obedience to an ancient instinct, after a summer in the stretches of the northland, the birds are migrating to their winter quarters.

How do birds know when to migrate? What profound, mysterious power exerts its strength? How do they recall the routes? We do not know. Through the long centuries, since the last ice sheet receded and left our sculptured landscape, wild geese have answered two powerful calls—northward in the spring and southward in the autumn.

October Glory

While bumblebee queens search for winter sanctuary and wood turtles dig into soft mud, the maples of America display their colors. On upland hillsides and mountain shoulders, along peaceful country roads and in valley woodlands, the maples make beauty for a few days in October.

We are told that the maple migrated long ago from western China across the Aleutians. No one knows how long the Indians had been using the sap of the maple for making syrup and sugar before the white man came to this continent. Maples are trees of the Northern Hemisphere: the red maple and the sugar, or rock maple, are the best known of the family, but silver or soft maples are found over a wide area in river bottoms. It is the silver maple that Lincoln knew along the valley of the Sangamon. There is a small trailing vine maple in British Columbia, and dwarf and Douglas maples in the West.

The sugar and the red maples are the ones that bring flaming glory to our landscape for a brief period. These friendly trees have beauty at all seasons of the year. A gaunt, old tree with deeply furrowed bark and huge gnarled limbs is a picture of strength and serenity; a sugar grove with scores or hundreds of maple trees is a temple of beauty when the leaves have turned crimson and gold.

October is also the time of the oaks' alpenglow, the second coloring that spreads soft hues and helps man ready himself for the white and gray of the winter. The oaks cling to their leaves long after the maples and birches, elms and alders, willows and larches have dropped their summer clothes. Perhaps it goes back to ancient eras when all oaks were evergreens and dropped their leaves a few at a time. After the last glacier retreated, the oaks worked northward, and now they are one of the important families of our region.

When we speak of oaks, we think of the massive and dignified white or black. They are indeed among the noblest of trees and have played an important role in our development. Strong white-oak timbers framed the sailing vessels that roamed the oceans; oak timbers have gone into houses and barns. The wood has been used for wagons and farm implements, for furniture and floors.

But there is another oak about which we read little and which, because of its small size, we ignore. This is the scrub oak, sometimes called the bear oak, because bears like to feed upon its small acorns. It is anyone's guess when a shrub ceases to be a shrub and becomes a tree, but most of the scrub oaks I have seen range from six or seven to perhaps twelve or fifteen feet in height. These are the oaks that make beauty on the uplands and sometimes in corners of fields and meadows. Go out on the hillsides on a mellow, sun-bright, tenth-month day and you will see the alpenglow. A patch of scrub oaks is a picture of frost-softened hues of gold and wine, brown and russet, tan and purple, wine and saffron.

If you are a Thoreau fan, you know that the sage of Walden often spoke of the scrub oak as one of his favorite trees. It is scraggly, and angular with thick, short branches. Often the main stem or trunk is twisted as if by powerful winds. It reminds me of the small mountain trees that one sees at the timber line. The blossoms appear when the leaves are from a third to a half grown; the acorns are small and require two seasons to reach maturity.

Now the scrubs are having their moment of glory. They do not compete with the giants of the family, but for a few weeks before winter comes, the scrub oaks' alpenglow gives color to the autumn canvas.

The large shagbark is a ragged, rugged and distinguished patriarch of field and wood. Perhaps one would not include it among the most beautiful trees of America, but it is a tree rich in history and meaning; from early pioneering days until the metal and rubber era revolutionized the habits of a nation, the shagbark played a dependable, important role. It was an integral part of the nation's farm life, for the tough wood provided sturdy whiffle-trees for wagons, strong ax handles, hoe handles and spade handles. The slow-burning wood meant efficient fuel in fireplaces and stoves, and its pungent, aromatic smoke has helped to cure millions of hams and sides of bacon.

Thousands of boys and girls have gathered the sweet-flavored nuts of this tree; and usually it is a tight race between young folks and the squirrels. As soon as a killing October frost has loosened the brown nuts and started them falling to the ground, a twelve-year-old has to be ready. Especially after a high wind, he wants to get to his favorite trees in a hurry, for the squirrels are working in high gear, caching food supplies for winter. Each year large shagbarks grow fewer as men cut them for lumber; but there are still many of these strong and rugged trees left in the bottomlands and on rich upland sites.

Water Witch

It was a bleak, raw and cold-wind day. Nimbus clouds were a heavy blanket between earth and sky; spits of driving rain swept across the countryside. Tall elms around the house and barn were whipped by sudden, powerful gusts. The group of men and boys behind the big barn were strangely uneasy. Alter-nately moving and quiet, they waited for the old man who had the mysterious power with the hazel wand. The farmer had de-cided to dig a well. It had been a long drought and he wanted a well near the barn. Men liked to watch Old Mose use the divining rod.

It was a scene of Biblical simplicity that dark day. One could feel the tension of the group as they waited. The laughter was forced and men spoke alternately too loudly or almost in a whisper. Then Old Mose came plodding up the road. He came through the gap in the wall. He was old and stooped. A heavy, ancient overcoat came almost to his boots. His rheumy eyes cir-cled the group. He held a forked branch in his hand.

The farmer spoke quietly. He told Old Mose he would like to dig a well near the barn. The old man said nothing. Then he began to walk back and forth. The men watched him carefully; no one paid any attention as a sudden gust of hard, cold rain pelted down.

Old Mose moved slowly through the stubble, his tattered coat flapping in the wind. He held the wand by the two prongs at arm's length. His eyes were on the ground; beads of sweat were glistening on his forehead. Then suddenly we saw it happen. As he came toward us, slowly the point of the stick turned down. The old man stopped. He backed up; he moved a bit to one side. Down went the point and men braced themselves in sympathy as the power of the pull fought the strength in the water witch's arms.

The point was straight down. The old man stopped. Slowly he released one side of the wand. He lifted an arm and rubbed it across his eyes. He looked around for the farmer. "Dig here," he said. Then he started back to the road—an old, old man in a long, dark coat.

Saturday Chores

The Standard Cider Mill, according to the catalog, was "positively the best hand cider mill on the market." The framework was oak; the mill parts were cast iron and steel and the press screw was steel. It was back-geared and had a heavy-bearing balance wheel. "You cannot buy an easier running, better finished or stronger hand mill at any price. Weight 190 lbs. Price $8.75."

When I was a boy, many general farmers figured on making a few barrels of cider each fall for prime vinegar come summer. Men differed as to which apples made the best-flavored vinegar, but Father always insisted that a half-and-half combination of Russets and Northern Spies produced a hearty tang and zip that could not be surpassed by other varieties.

After the apples were sorted in late fall, a lad knew he was in for a hard Saturday's work. Apples were first finely ground in the wooden hopper on top, and then the juicy mush was pushed down into the tub; next the threaded press screw was turned down by its iron knobs. The screw forced a tight wooden cover against the pomace. Theoretically a lad was supposed to turn the screw hard enough to squeeze out the last bit of juice which dropped into the half hogshead below. Cranking the grinder was not too difficult, but tightening the press screw was a horse of another color. Just when a fellow figured he could not exert another ounce of strength, Father would come along, glance at the length of threading above the bar and say, "Better give it a few more turns, son. There's still some juice in the pomace." At that point a lad had to refresh himself with a few sips of the sweet cider through an oat straw, and then he had the strength to make another turn or two.

Time was when a farmer with a few acres of field corn felt he had a real job ahead when it came time to shock it. Today, modern science makes it possible to plant, cultivate, harvest and shell corn by machinery. But fifty years ago, many farm lads knew what one of their jobs would be in October.

Only one who has shocked corn appreciates that it is boring work. You bend down, cut an armful of stalks, straighten up and carry a load to the spot where the shock will stand. Most men prefer to make four sizable armfuls into one shock, with the bases of the stalks spread out to give a firm foundation. Around the upper middle, you used twine or a strip of hemlock bark to tie the four sections tightly together. You sometimes had a little difficulty with the shocks until you got the hang of it. But then the work went pretty fast, and there was a certain satisfaction in knowing that you only had to do it once a year.

A few farmers still appreciate that for best flavor, potatoes should be left to "ripen" a bit in the soil after the tops of the vines are brown and shriveled. There is still life in the roots and it is nature's particular method of maturing a product so that it will keep. Furthermore, if the potatoes are left a spell, they acquire a flavor that you won't find in spuds dug before the vines are barely browned. My father was all for letting potatoes ripen. And the longer the better as far as I was concerned. But eventually the time came when I had to go out after breakfast on a Saturday morning to dig the Green Mountains, Rural New Yorkers and Irish Cobblers with a potato hook.

On a brisk day in early October, digging potatoes was not a bad job. A boy had a chance to watch birds flying over the field, to study flaming colors on the hillsides, and to listen to the chickadee's cheerful call from the edge of the woodland. Sometimes a plump, philosophical-looking woodchuck came from his den as the sun climbed its arc and flooded the countryside with warmth; the solemn chuck sat for an hour surveying the scene like a benign and tolerant elder statesman. At mid-afternoon it was time to pick the spuds into baskets and pour them into burlap bags, so Father could haul them to the barn floor for sorting later in the fall. Not exciting work, but somehow satisfying; and a fourteen-year-old realized when day was done and the hilltops were lighted at dusk that he had helped harvest one of the year's important crops.

There was one muscle-wearying task at the turn of the century that I dreaded, and that was hay-baling. Father, along with other solid farmers, believed the secret of economic success was to raise a little more of everything than the livestock and family needed. He was especially proud of his big crops of hay. "You can't beat first class timothy and clover," he declared. "It's good for milkers, heifers, and horses." If a neighboring farmer ran short of hay, Father always planned to have a few extra tons available to sell for welcome cash.

For a small pressing job, a Kenwood Hand Hay Press was used, a diabolical machine, to a lad's mind. "No farm can be considered complete without it," the catalog said. "It is cheap at $24.45, compact, powerful and practical. One man and a boy can bale from two to three tons per day, turning out bales that weigh from 80 to 100 pounds. The lever which operates the plunger is 8 feet long. A weight of 100 pounds on the end of the lever gives a pressure of about 10 tons on the plunger. No more useful machine can be placed on the farm. Weight 425 pounds. Price $24.45."

No matter what the catalog said, I never believed I could exert ten tons' pressure. It was hard, dusty, unrelenting work to pitch hay down from the scaffold, cram it into the baling chamber, shove down on the lever and then keep repeating the process until the chamber was full. The corrugated chamber prevented the hay from springing back when the lever was raised for a new batch of hay. Optimism is an admirable trait, in advertising and otherwise, but a lad and his father never seemed to be able to get more than a ton baled between chore times on a Saturday. Hand baling of hay is one of the many tasks of yesteryear now done by mechanical power. A boy knew that the baled hay meant cash money for needed farm and family purchases, but when Father finally decided enough had been baled, it was always welcome news.

Country Lane

A country lane is one of the most appealing of nature's pictures. It is homey and intimate. It does not have the grandeur of ledge-topped mountains nor the sweep of evergreen hillsides. But somehow man frequently appreciates the small and familiar more than he does the grand and awesome.

A country lane is not a public way. It is a private, personal path or road. You see them leading from barnyards to pastures; they branch from dirt roads and lead across fields and meadows. They climb pasture hillsides to maple sugar groves and to wood-lots on a slope.

Now the walls and fences resemble gray stitching on the landscape. The birches, alders, hornbeams, and sumacs are feathery; birds' nests are wind-torn blotches. The gray paper cones of hornets' nests swing at the tips of supple branches. Goldenrod heads are gray and bleached and tall stalks of mullein stand above frost-brown grasses.

Walk a country lane on a golden day in October. Away from the sound of traffic, a man can feel the assurance that a peaceful environment brings. He can enjoy that poignant period in the fall when the countryside is again revealed after the hardwoods and shrubs have dropped their leaves.

The Skunk That Couldn't

It happened this way. Our region was a famous apple growing section of southern New Hampshire. The apple growers set out young trees, called whips. These whips were straight stems, and as they grew the orchardists pruned them to start evenly spaced branches around the stems or trunks. The bark of the young whips is succulent and a favorite food of rabbits, so orchardists paid boys 25 cents for each rabbit they caught in box traps. Around 1910, this trapping was an important source of income for a considerable number of boys in town. We needed revenue when it came time for the mail-order list.

A box trap, for the benefit of those who are not familiar with them, is a wooden box with a trigger on which an apple is stuck. When an animal eats the apple, the trigger is loosened from its catch. This trigger is attached by a string to the lifted door at the front of the box. When the apple is jarred loose, the front of the box drops and the animal is captured.

I shall always remember the day it happened. Eddie was ahead of me as he stepped up to a box trap and peered through the slit in the top. He jumped backward fast and looked at me. "It's a skunk," he said.

Then it dawned on us. We looked at each other. There was no scent.

There are many things in life that generate uncertainty, but there is one fact about skunks that is certain. When you catch one in a trap, there is ample fragrance. If you have had experience with skunks, you know what is meant. Skunk aroma is distinctive; it is powerful; it lasts a long time. Most important of all if you decided to specialize in skunks, don't believe the saying that you are safe once a skunk has let go with its spray. I have seen a skunk spray three or four times in rapid succession when its temper was roiled.

To get back to Eddie and me, after we were absolutely sure that we had a skunk that couldn't, we carried the box trap home and put it on the upper scaffold of the horse barn, where hardly anyone went except ourselves. We snitched doughnuts, cake, and cookies. We took cream and milk from the milk house. We named our skunk Julius.

It may be difficult to believe, but in a few days Julius was as friendly as a house cat. He came to us eagerly when we brought food. Julius was fat and sleek and he liked to be picked up and to snuggle in our arms. We could not decide what to do with him, and we discussed the possibilities. We could, of course, take him to school and start a commotion. We could take him to the general store on Saturday evening when a big crowd was doing the weekly trading. We could even wait until Town Meeting and start another American Revolution.

Then fate stepped in as it often does and the situation resolved itself. In those days the local Grange, Patrons of Husbandry, No. 33, would hold open meetings to which everyone in town was invited. After a bountiful country supper, everyone went upstairs to the large hall for the program of recitations, piano selections, solos, duets, and the inevitable reminiscences of Deacon Ward.

The Grange decided to have an open meeting and asked Teacher to put on the program with the eighth-grade pupils. So Teacher arranged for the usual list of events and asked me what I would do.

"I'll give a nature talk," I said, "and I'll work up something with Eddie."

Eddie and I made our plans. The evening came and we had a big supper and everyone was in a genial mood. We went upstairs and it came time for the program. We had Julius in a box. No one thought a thing about it. Perhaps they thought we had rocks, birds' nests, or something else to go with the talk when it came my turn.

After some girls recited and played the piano, Teacher said, "Haydn and Eddie will now give a nature talk."

I stood up and said, "I'm going to give you a little talk about skunks." Eddie sat on a chair beside me, wooden-faced. "This is a serious subject," I said, "and I hope you will treat it as such." I saw the smiles on the faces of some of the younger men, fellows from twenty to thirty. What was the minister's son up to now? For a panicky moment I wondered what would happen to Eddie and me after it was over.

"We have decided this is to be an illustrated lecture," I said, and turned to Eddie. He reached into the box and passed Julius up to me. For an instant the hall was absolutely quiet.

"I'll come to you and you can pass Julius around," I said.

I started toward the young children in the front row. Then the shrieks and screams began. Men and women stood up.

I walked slowly forward, Eddie by my side. I held Julius out so everyone could see him. All was going according to plan. Slowly we edged forward while folks shouted and called and pressed toward the door and then down the stairs.

No one dared touch me. If anyone started toward me, I held Julius out with his rear toward the enemy. It was a battle of wills but Eddie and I slowly got away. And you may be sure we did not return.

We wondered what our punishment would be. The next day I heard Father call Eddie's dad. They had quite a conversation. Finally I heard Father laugh and I knew the sun would continue to smile.

We kept Julius on the scaffold until spring. Teacher even had us bring him to school and I gave a serious talk on skunks. In the spring we let Julius go in the woodland where we caught him. A skunk is really an interesting pet, but if you get one just be sure he can't.

The Fringe-Top Surrey

To understand the place of the fringe-top surrey in rural economy half a century and more ago, let me explain a bit about the vehicles used by the average, reasonably prosperous farmer.

The democrat wagon was the backbone of country road travel. This was a plain, utilitarian wagon with a box body, four sturdy wheels, heavy springs, two seats, and a vertical dashboard. This was the most common wagon on New Hampshire farms. It carried six people, three to a seat. You could remove the rear seat if you needed to bring home a few milk jugs from the village depot, or a couple of bags of cottonseed meal. The democrat was a strong, dependable wagon.

Then there was the top buggy, useful for carrying one or two persons. It was fancier than the democrat and had springs with a bit more flexibility. In the democrat, you received a solid, jarring jounce when you hit a half buried rock in the road. Another important point to a farm lad was that Father rarely wanted the democrat washed. But he expected the top buggy to shine.

For a while, we had a buckboard, and in many ways it was

my favorite, a one-seat vehicle with a low-slung, very springy body. As I drove Belle to the village, the springs were so flexible that you floated over the bumps and humps in the wheel tracks. I can still see our buckboard. It was a battered affair that Father bought at an auction. I never had to wash it. The only maintenance was to grease the axles occasionally.

That was the equipment we had for a few years. Then a fringe-top surrey came into our lives. To us, and the community, it meant we had taken a step up the social and economic ladder. Keep in mind that a man paid off the mortgage and had a reasonable nest egg incubating in the bank before he bought such a luxury item as a surrey.

There was lively family discussion after Father said he guessed it was time for the Pearsons to get a fringe top. The mail-order catalog offered several, and each surrey had its distinctive features. Mother was all in favor of one of the less expensive models, but Father had a different idea. "Rosie," he said, "if we can afford a fringe-top surrey at all, we can afford a fairly good one. We won't get the most expensive one, but neither are we going to get a cheap one. We want all the trimmings if we're going to ride in style."

The final choice was the Acme Royal Cut Surrey for $89.50. It was generous in size, with snappy-looking leather protectors above the rear wheels. Part of this leather protector or fender was the step to the rear seat. The seats were luxuriously upholstered with dark green English body cloth. The seat backs were regally high. The wheels, with their slender metal spokes and narrow rims, gave an aristocratic touch to the over-all picture. On each side of the front seat was a French oil-burning lamp. The body was a dark green color, and both the body and the wheel spokes were artistically decorated with narrow maroon stripes.

But the glory of that vehicle was the fringed top, supported by four steel rods. The top itself was solid, reinforced leather. The fringe hung from the edge of the top; it was long, rich and luxurious looking, bright red and lavishly trimmed with gold-braided cords and tassels.

It was a banner day in the Pearsons' lives when I hitched Belle to the surrey and we drove along the country road to the church in the village. We had kept things a secret, and eyes opened wide as I drove up to the granite step of the church. I pulled up with a flourish. Father helped Mother down. The sisters had their chins a bit higher than normal. I sat up very straight and drove Belle around back of the church and put her in one of the horse sheds.

I'll confess something. After the newness wore off, I made a painful discovery. Father was so proud of that surrey that he wanted it clean and sparkling all the time. That meant, literally, that I had to wash it and polish it after every trip to town. I suppose the moral of the story is, if you aspire to something above your neighbor's possessions, you pay a penalty. Probably that is why, in the following years, I was perfectly happy to drive the family in the democrat instead of the flossy fringe-top surrey.

Ingathering Time

After the first few light frosts have laid tentative, testing hands on the fields and gardens, there comes the time of ingathering. It is good to work in the garden on a sun-drenched, tenth-month day when the bluejays are winging above the sugar lot and smaller birds are singing in the old Russet tree at the end of the yard. It isn't necessarily glamorous work to fork out the carrots and beets; pulling the turnips and cabbages can become a bit monotonous. But there is a deep satisfaction in growing one's own food and storing it against the time of cold and snow.

Sometimes in a mild October a man can get an extra cutting of sweet, frost-limp rowen, and the tangy, nostril-tingling fragrance of new-mown hay fills the air. It is good to harvest the Greenings and Northern Spies, Blue Pearmains and Kings from the old orchard on the hillside. A man takes satisfaction in looking at the vegetables and fruits in the earthen-floored house cellar. The bins of Green Mountains, the boxes of fruit, the shelves of fruits and vegetables, the jars of jams and jellies paint a picture in the soft glow of the lantern.

Ingathering is a special time of year. As the colors flame on the hills and the bonfires of autumn burn out, as bare trees make etchings on the ridges and the goldenrod turns into gray ghosts along the roadsides, the countryman works along at his harvesting and gets ready for the winter. Ingathering means a harvest of material things, but as the fall edges along toward colder weather, one also feels that he had harvested a crop for the heart.

Foretelling Winter Weather

To farmers and countrymen, the weather is an intimate, almost personal matter. The better they can read nature's signs the more efficiently they can plan their work. In my mind's eye, I can still see Father pause on the way across the farmyard to do morning chores and stop a minute to study the weather signs. He could read the mountains' prophecy; he understood the direction of the wind and its influence on the next day or so. On a winter's day he studied the sky and read the clouds' message. In the summer, in haying time, he watched the mists on the meadow, and he would tell me that if the mists began to rise by seven, we would have a good haying day

Many of the old sayings were based on experiences that had been passed down through the generations. We moderns are likely to dismiss them as folklore, but in reality they were based on valid observations and confirmed by long repetition. At sunset when Mother looked to Bald Mountain and saw a red ball of sun she would say, "Red at night, sailor's delight; red in the morning, sailors take warning." In the spring and summer, it was a sign of good weather if dew were heavy, and the droplets of water on the grass glistened like jewels in the sun. "When the dew is on the grass, rain will never come to pass." Another jingle that comes to mind from boyhood days goes this way. "When the morn is dry, rain is nigh. When the morn is wet, no rain you get." The Indians told white men that if the moon had a ring about it, rain would come soon.

In this region, I depend a good deal in the summer on the succession of cloud formations. Big, fluffy cumulus clouds are a sign of fair weather. Then in succession we are likely to have cirrus, stratus, and nimbus. Nimbus are the dark, low-lying, threatening clouds which bring our storms. There are many variations and subdivisions of the four main groups, but I have noticed this succession of cloud types over the years.

Each October, I come out with my forecast for the winter. Let's say the signs point toward a humdinger—one of the coldest and snowiest winters in a generation. Here is the way I tell. The cattail heads are very long and a deeper chocolate-brown color than normal. Onion skins are unusually thick and tough, and the husks on the corn are very tightly bound to the cobs. Down in the swamps the muskrats have built their igloos tall and the cocoons on reeds are high above the expected snow level.

Perhaps you have noticed in some autumns that the pine trees shed many more brown needles than usual. This is nature's way of thinning the foliage so that heavy snows will not break so many branches. If a severe winter is ahead, paper hornets build their conical gray nests high on the branches of gray birches and alders. The wild geese go south early and you hear their haunting cries as they wing across the sky on a starlit night.

I also judge by the colors of the lichens on old wooden posts and stone walls and on the north side of old oaks and beeches in the woodland. You will notice that in the early autumn the color of the lacy tracings begins to deepen. The greens become greener, and the pale gray of many lichens changes to a deeper hue.

Some of the old-timers believe that a coon's fur is a reliable barometer. All these signs have their degree of validity; all have a place in my thinking. But now I want to tell you the best way of all to foretell winter weather. I'll admit I have not convinced my peers; but on the other hand they have not convinced me I am wrong.

I judge by the chipmunks' tails. You should begin to watch the little fellows in September. They often estivate in the heat and humidity of August, but when the cooler, brisker days come, they wake up and begin to prepare for winter. Then if a chipmunk carries its tail floating to the rear, it means an easy winter. If the tail is carried straight up and down, it means a normal cold season. But if the chipmunks carry their tails far over their backs pointing in the direction they are traveling, that means an old-fashioned winter with deep snow, many periods of zero weather, and high winds—the type of winter that Grandpa likes to describe.

My advice to all, when the chipmunks carry their tails over their backs, is to buy some extra heavy long ones, make sure you have plenty of hay for the cows, and see that the woodshed is heaped high with good dry wood.

NOVEMBER

LONG AGO, NOVEMBER BECAME THE DROVER'S MONTH TO farmers in Maine, New Hampshire, and Vermont. Drovers, or cattle buyers, came into the back country farming regions and bought beef cattle for the city markets to the south. A buyer collected a herd to drive over the road to Brighton, Springfield, or Portland, and made a dicker with a farmer in central spots to keep the cattle fed and watered as he traveled a region and bought a few steers from individual farmers. When the herd was collected, a buyer often hired a lad or two to help him drive the beeves to market. Along the road over which the herds were prodded, certain farms and taverns were well known as places to bed down for the night. Not only were cattle driven to market in November, but I have read old accounts of turkey drives in which hundreds of the big birds were driven over country roads to market.

There are some who do not like the eleventh month. It is an in-between season in nature. The seeds of trees, shrubs and grasses have matured, the year's crops have been harvested. Brown is the color of the landscape, and the grasses on upland fields and meadow mowings are frost-drained.

It is a time of simplicity. A man can walk his fields and woodlands and see much that his eyes missed in the lushness of summer. Weather-furrowed stone walls show clearly on the hillsides; maples are silhouetted at flaming sunset on granite ridges; bare, tall elms in the river valleys reach above the cold, gray water of slow-moving rivers and brooks. Tattered nests of warblers and vireos tell where bird families were raised; gray paper hornets' nests swing from birch branches. Along the stone walls one comes upon mounds of tan soil where woodchucks had their dens.

November can, and usually does, give us a mixture of weather. There are beautiful, sunny days when the temperature climbs into the fifties. Mornings are cold and crisp, and the fields are powdered with gray-white frost. At high noon, warmth broods over the fields and hills. By mid-afternoon, shadows creep down the hillsides and night falls abruptly. When a man comes in from evening chores and stops a minute in the farmyard to smell the air, the sky is blazing with stars. "Clear and cold again tonight" he thinks, and is grateful for the shed full of good, dry hardwood.

November is the brown month. November is the time of preparation for winter. Man cannot choose his seasons but he can, if he will, take each as a part of his experience and from each gain something to enrich his life.

Indian Summer

Whenever one attempts to discuss New England weather, he is certain to run into opposition. Apart from personal opinions about foods, I have discovered no subject about which my peers are so opinionated, dogmatic and closed-minded as they are concerning weather. Therefore, when I say, as I must, because I believe in honest, objective reporting, that Indian Summer never comes until well into November, I know there will be disagreement.

Various explanations have been offered as to the origin of the term "Indian Summer." Some colonials believed that the fires set by Indians in the fall caused the hazy smokiness that lingers on our hills and mountains when the warmth of this period hovers over the land. The Reverend James Freeman, the first Unitarian minister of King's Chapel, Boston, wrote in 1812, "Two or three weeks of fair weather in which the air is perfectly transparent, and the clouds which float in a sky of purest azure, are adorned with brilliant colors. This charming season is called the Indian Summer." The earliest reference I know is that by Crèvecoeur who wrote in 1778 that winter snow is "often preceded by a short interval of smoke and mildness, called the Indian Summer."

Just when the few days, or occasionally a week or two, of the relaxing warmth will come to New England is anyone's guess. But it won't be true Indian Summer until we have had Squaw Winter—that period of cold blustering winds, snow squalls, sleet, and cold rain that play tick-tack on the farm shop windows. According to some, the term "Indian" in Indian Summer has approximately the same meaning as "Indian" in Indian giver—something given for a period but likely to be quickly and unpredictably snatched away.

After the eleventh month has worked along, and after a period of stormy weather, Indian Summer will come. You will feel it in the soft breeze that pushes in from the southwest; you'll see it in the purple-smoky haze that hangs over frost-brown fields and uplands; you can feel it when you walk your acres on a warm day that reminds you of early September.

It may be that Indian Summer is a bonus given us to recompense for Squaw Winter; it may be the weatherman wishes to give dilatory citizens a second chance to catch up on essential fall work. But I am grateful for these few days of warmth and sunshine and agree with the poet who said that whatever the reason for Indian Summer, it is "real summer, briefly reborn."

Woodland Ravine

Since boyhood days I have liked ravines. A ravine, according to the dictionary, is a depression worn out by running water, larger than a gully and smaller than a valley. Now that autumn is working down the steep slide toward winter, it is good to know a ravine where you can get away from the rush and roar of daily routine.

Our varied topography in New England is due to the action of the great ice sheets that bludgeoned and harrowed the region. It was perhaps 500 million years ago in the Cambrian Era that the

Berkshires, White Mountains and Green Mountains were lifted above the seething waters of an ancient ocean. Dinosaurs once roamed what is now the Connecticut Valley. Our Mount Monadnock is a picturesque mountain, and the word monadnock has come to mean a hill standing by itself.

The great ice cap left ponds and lakes; it filled lowlands with good soil and scraped soil from the uplands. It carved cliffs and ridges, swamps and depressions. And it left ravines. Clearwater brooks sing down the floor of the ravines; ferns lean over the water, and when the water falls over a granite shelf, the ferns in season wave in the moving air above the foaming bubbles.

It is pleasant to sit on a sunny November day on the side of a ravine. The leaves have fallen from the maples, birches, and beeches, and the leaf carpet on the ravine sides is as soft-hued as an antique, oriental rug. Only a few weeks ago all was shadowy, cool and moist. Now the ravine is open to the sun and the granite edgings are warm in the slanting rays. Last spring, the brook at the bottom was a leaping, singing stream, swollen by melted snow, hurrying downward to a meadow stream. Now it is a small, quiet trickle, flowing unhurriedly over gravel and smooth stones.

Stump-Sitting

There is one neglected leisure-time activity I would respectfully call to your attention. Very few citizens have taken up stump-sitting as a regular hobby. Its advantages are obvious if you consider them objectively. First of all, pondering the present high cost of living, it is an inexpensive hobby. Second, you can locate a favorite stump in a pleasant woodland, and always know where to go. Third, though you use the same stump through the months and years, the rewards are always interesting and different. Equipment is simple. You need warm clothes and warm footwear, and it is helpful to have a pair of field glasses and a hand lens. Other than this, the chief requirements for successful stump sitting are reasonably good eyesight and an interest in nature.

Forty years of serious and purposeful stump-sitting have

taught me a few other points that may be helpful to beginners in this avocation. Choose a stump in a protected clearing, preferably with evergreens on the north and west to break the wind. It is good to have open woods of deciduous trees before you, for the sake of vista and perspective. For comfort's sake, the stump should be reasonably level. Experienced stump-sitters have been known to place old pillows or folded burlap bags on the stump.

The witch hazel tree provides the stump-sitter with a few pleasant surprises in the fall. The Onondaga Indians called witch hazel "spotted stick" because the older canes of the shrub turn a weathered, irregularly dotted yellow and tan in autumn. At about the same time, when other flowers and shrubs are dormant, the witch hazel shakes out its narrow, yellow-ribbon blossoms in clumps of three or four. The oval leaves turn a dull gold and drop quickly; but the blossoms keep their rich color for three or four weeks. A plant that blossoms in November in the north temperate region is unusual enough, but the witch hazel is not content with that one trait; it is probably best known for the fragrant extract that is distilled from its roots.

Perhaps, as some claim, the witch hazel gets its name from the fact that pioneers used the forked brush of the shrub as a divining rod to locate water. It does not matter, for the spotted stick is an unorthodox personality in its own right.

Another interesting tree for the stump-sitter is the tamarack or hacmatac, a deciduous conifer. It is a tree of the colder regions, and when winter draws near, the bright, blue-green leaves, or needles, change to a pale golden ochre. After a brief period the golden needles fall to the ground.

The tamarack is not so striking a tree, perhaps, as the white pine or the spruce. It is usually from thirty to fifty feet high, with slender branches that sometimes droop in long graceful curves. It is thinly foliaged compared with other conifers. In early April the seed-bearing flowers on the branch tips are a glowing, rich red hue. Cones are short and chubby and often remain on the tree for a year after the seeds have dropped. In the lowland woods on a sunny November day you will see the golden needles of the tamarack shining in the thin sunlight. It is a picturesque tree, fragile and dainty in contrast with its needled cousins. For a fortnight or more after the hardwoods have dropped their foliage, the tamarack comes into its own, adding the afterglow of November.

Autumn Pies

One good reason for living in the United States is the long list of pies from which a man can choose. We do not say that cakes, puddings, and cookies should not be readily available—especially chewy, nutty cookies. But after all, as most men know, there is nothing better with which to conclude all three meals of the day, and nothing more satisfying for a snack at bedtime than a quarter of a good-sized, deep, juicy pie.

Now there is some difference of opinion about having pie for breakfast, but as far as I'm concerned there is no better way to start off the day. I do not claim that pie for breakfast would stave off all irritations and frustrations, but it is more than a fitting conclusion to the day's first meal. Most people lie abed a whiffle too long in the morning, and then start the day in a frantic dissipation of energy. If everyone would get up a half-hour earlier, we would all have time for a piece of pie and learn to start the day off right. The best pie for breakfast at this time of year is fresh apple pie. And, of course, pie for breakfast should always be well heated in the oven.

There is also some difference of opinion about the merits of squash *vs.* pumpkin pie. There is no question in my mind that a pumpkin pie has certain qualities not possessed by a squash pie. The pumpkin's advantage is slight, but there is just a dite more flavor, an intangible, mouth-watering deliciousness that is never achieved by the squash.

Many farmers formerly grew pumpkins in the cornfield and harvested them in the fall to feed to the cows and pigs. It was not a genuine Halloween unless a lad had a prize pumpkin to carve with his cherished Northland Trapper's Four Bladed Knife. A pumpkin's most fortunate destiny, naturally, is in a good pie. With plenty of creamy milk, and the right combination of cinnamon, nutmeg, ginger and cloves, a pumpkin can ask for nothing finer. I hope those who have so polemically clung to their ideas about squash pie will see the light and insist on pumpkin pie this year.

Making Land

Father and I "made" land in the late fall before the earth was locked tight. We lumbered off a small area and planned to pull the stumps and get rid of the rocks and stones. It wasn't a large-scale operation, but even a quarter-acre of good soil was important on a hillside general farm.

It was good work on a pleasant Saturday just before winter. Father was a master craftsman at adjusting chains around a stump so the team of big workhorses could exert maximum leverage. Their powerful flank muscles rippled as they leaned into the collars. Usually the stump came out with a ripping, tearing noise; but it would not give. The horses knew when to let up. That meant more digging and chopping a root or two. It was slow work, but as Father used to say, "There are some jobs where it doesn't pay to hurry."

Countrymen on hillside farms who still pick stones know there is one crop which never fails. Whether you plow in spring or autumn, nature, from some mysterious but never-failing source, always comes through with a bountiful crop of stones to be hauled off on the battered, splintered old stoneboat. Big rocks were pried onto the stoneboat; small rocks were tossed on, and then the load was carried to the stone pile at the low end of the field.

There has been considerable controversy over the terms "stoneboat" *versus* "stone drag." The first term is correct; it probably originated because the upturned prow resembled to a degree the front end of a boat. Also, with some imagination, you can say the stoneboat glides over the land as a boat glides through water. The average size of stoneboats is about six feet long and four feet wide.

There is a logical technique to loading a stoneboat. Larger rocks are placed around the sides and across the ends and the inside is filled with smaller stones. When the boat was loaded, it was fun to stand on it, start up the team and head for the big stone pile at the edge of a field. If the pile were out of sight of the house, a lad could set up a target on the heap and use the smaller stones for ammunition.

But the part I enjoyed most was driving the team to the stump fence with the stump and its tangled roots jerking and leaping at the end of the chain. A stump fence isn't neat and orderly like a three-wire fence, a woven-wire boundary or a single-strand electric fence. But it has intangible values never found in metal boundaries. Birds build their nests among the tangled roots; woodchucks dig their dens in its protection, and snakes are partial to the area. A farm lad liked to work on a Saturday at building a stump fence. It was exciting to see the stumps and roots come out; it was fun to handle the horses, and a boy knew that come spring he would enjoy exploring along a fence that offered sanctuary to wildlife.

Fall plowing always went hand in hand with making land. Of all the inventions conceived in the mind of man and executed through his powers of reasoning, few are more important than the plow. Many a good farmer still believes in fall plowing and today leaves his furrows so the soil will not erode from rain. Plowing is more than a routine operation. There is something fundamentally satisfying about stirring the soil. I remember walking behind Old Jerry on a crisp November afternoon, my hands on the curved wooden plow handles, the reins over my shoulders. Old Jerry understood the job, and would give a kindly snort as he stopped and turned at furrow's end.

Barn Chores

I wish more men had the pleasant experience of sitting on a solid milking stool twice a day. There are, as you would expect, differing opinions among farmers as to the best type of stool. The three-legged variety is the most common, but there are a few courageous souls who enjoy living dangerously and actually seem to prefer a one-legged stool. As for me, I want both solidity and comfort. Most men agree, however, that the seat should be of polished hardwood; a seat made of splintery hemlock or fir offers obvious dangers. And the legs should extend at a considerable angle to furnish mental comfort. Even on a four-legged stool, if the legs are vertical, a sudden sideways thrust can cause a man to lose his dignity—and the milk. Another good idea is to pad the seat with a couple of inches of old patchwork quilt. No reason to be Spartan. It will, of course, cause some comment, but think of it this way. If you milk a cow twice a day from the time you are ten to the time you are sixty, you will sit down on that milking stool 36,500 times. That's a lot of down-sitting—and you may as well be as comfortable as possible.

Sweeping up in the barn was the last chore I had to do before supper on a November evening. A birch broom was used for that purpose, and Father and I used to make them ourselves in the farm shop. I don't suppose anyone makes birch brooms any more, but on a raw, rainy, November day when the cluttered farm shop was a comfortable eighty degrees from the fire in the old stove, I used to spend a pleasant hour or two fashioning a broom which I could use in the tie-up and barn during the months ahead.

Along in the middle fall, Father and I cut a good supply of supple, slender branches of gray or white birch. We tossed them in a heap beneath the work bench where they dried out and waited for the day when we used them. The two secrets of a top-notch birch broom are care in selecting the eighteen-inch-long branches, and patience in fitting them evenly around a maple-sapling handle. I liked to have about a six-inch overlap around the handle, so the sweeping ends would be firmly held by the strong cord. That gave twelve inches of elastic branch for the actual sweeping end of the broom. It was slow work, for each branch had to be cut exactly the right length and the whole bundle had to be round, evenly spaced, and very tight around the handle. But on a cold eleventh-month day, with a northeast wind moaning in the chimney and brittle sleet clicking against the window panes, I wasn't in any particular hurry to leave the shop. It wasn't fancy work, but when the tool was finished, I knew it was an honest job and would serve its purpose well for months to come.

The Sleepers

All forms of life must adjust to their environment, or they must change their environment to fit their special needs. No phenomenon of nature is more awe-inspiring than hibernation—that mysterious and efficient method of surviving a time of low temperatures and scarcity of food.

A snail manufactures a membrane at the open end of its shell, and lives a semi-death until the soil warms again. Chipmunks curl up in their nests below the frost line. Red squirrels and grays sleep for long periods in the coldest weather, but come out in thawing spells. Naturalists sometimes speak of the seven sleepers—the bat, bear, woodchuck, racoon, skunk, chipmunk, and jumping mouse.

There are many points concerning hibernation that scientists are still exploring. One of the many misconceptions is that the animals live during the winter on the fat they have stored during the fall. We watch squirrels dashing about in late September and during October; we see lazy woodchucks in the clover patches and we naturally assume they are growing fat so they can use this for food during the cold time. But biologists agree, in general, that the fat stored is not for winter use; it is for food in early spring when animals emerge from the long sleep, and food is not readily available.

One of the phenomena that has interested me since boyhood days is the way a colony of honeybees survives the winter. The workers continue to store honey until cold weather. Then the colony clusters in the middle of the hive with the queen in the center. Through the late fall and the winter there is constant motion in the cluster of bees. The outside bees push into the center. If there is sufficient food stored, the colony lives through the winter. If you have opened a colony on a mild winter day, you may have been surprised at the activity. On a high-temperature day, the bees may take "cleansing" flights to rid themselves of waste food. A strong colony will survive weather far below zero if food is available.

From a tiny bee to a fat woodchuck is a jump, but while the bee may keep up a minimum of activity, moving in and out of the cluster, a woodchuck really goes to sleep. Four or five feet beneath the ground, he curls up in his nest pocket. The temperature of his blood may drop to forty degrees, and his pulse may go as low as twelve beats an hour. In late February, he usually awakens and goes searching for a mate.

Now that the nights are chilly and the ground is beginning to harden, the turtles and frogs, bumblebees and bears, the timber rattlesnakes, raccoons, chipmunks, bats, skunks and snails are getting ready for their long winter nap. Perhaps these animals have the right idea. I do not completely understand the mystery of hibernation, but I know that nature sometimes has a wisdom beyond the ken of man.

Smoke from Farm Chimneys

Half a century ago smoke spiraled from farmhouse chimneys, and a good countryman watching the plumes rise and drift away calculated the weather from the smoke's behavior.

Forehanded farmers were proud of their woodsheds come November, and felt a glow of satisfaction as they came in from evening chores and let soft lantern light play on the high-stacked tiers. Solid, dry wood gave a gray-purple smoke, and the column above the chimney was a badge that stamped a man. A billow of dark, heavy smoke meant that a woman was struggling to bake with green wood. An old country proverb says there are always those who try to live on love and green wood.

There are men and women living in teeming cities who remember the smell of woodsmoke in the air on a gray, brooding autumn day. Boys and girls tramping a mile or two to District School took for granted the smoke that curled upward, hesitated, and then drifted away—a hyphen on a page of time. Each year the smoke columns become fewer as gas, oil, and electricity decrease man's labors. However, when one rides the country roads he still sees an occasional banner above a red chimney. One cannot check the tide of progress—and would not if he could. But we wish that all realized the deep meaning of smoke rising from a farmhouse chimney.

Extended Architecture

I am in favor of expansion houses. This usually means that a man can finish off a room or two upstairs if he needs or wishes to. But what I really favor is a house with a long ell that connects with the barn. If you had the good fortune to be raised on a north-country farm, and if the farmstead was an example of extended architecture, you know how satisfying it was to be able to go from the kitchen to the cow barn and not freeze to death. When a bitter winter wind is sweeping down from the north and driving snow against the buildings, a man is grateful for the foresight of his ancestors.

All over the north country you see these extended houses. Sometimes they form one long building with a straight roof line —a building divided into sections for woodshed, tool house, carriage shed, and farm shop. Sometimes there is a series of miniature barns with a serrated roof line. Usually the smaller buildings lead to a large barn at the end of the line. The basic principle is the same. It is a form of architecture fitted to the needs of our climate. The connected house, ell, and barn of the Northeast is a transplant from England. The early colonists were familiar with the English plan of a covered walk or shed that led from the manor house to barns, stables, and woodsheds.

When we came to our farm in Hancock in 1908, we had a good example of extended architecture in an almost classic pattern. The story-and-a-half Cape Codder nestled under a huge, old sugar maple. At the foot of the sloping lawn, a clear-water brook sang on its way from the mountain behind the house to the larger stream in the meadow. The summer kitchen with its granite doorsteps, iron kettle in brick arch and spacious pantry was attached to the main house. From the summer kitchen there extended a series of sheds, one for the wood, one for wagons and sleighs, and one for the farm shop. From the last shed we went directly into the big, long cow barn.

The big barn was set at a right angle to the long ell. The barn ran east and west. The big doors through which we drove with loads of hay were north and south, so when we came in with a load we had to turn west and go up a slope around the horse barn after unloading. The horse barn formed the third side of the barnyard.

It wasn't long after we came to the farm that Father decided the situation was dangerous. A fire could wipe out all the buildings; therefore we took down part of the ell. He also decided that we did not need a separate horse barn and we remodeled one end of the cow barn and made stalls for the horses.

I have seen examples of extended architecture where a pen for the hens was built onto the south or east side of a barn, with a door to the pen opening from the cow barn. I have also seen lean-tos for a pig pen attached to the main barn. In olden days it was also common to keep the pigs in the barn cellar in the section where the horse manure was collected. On Glenrose Farm, however, Father would not consider such a thing. We had a spacious yard with a small, tight, low-roofed building for the pigs. In the fall and winter, until butchering time, one of my tasks was to keep the building stuffed with hay. The two pigs we raised burrowed into the hay for warmth.

As I recall, the first year or so we kept a dozen or more hens under the scaffold at the west end of the barn, but it quickly became evident that they raised too much dust. So we built a henhouse about a hundred feet behind the house, and I can remember well going up to the house just at dark during the winter to empty the water vessels. If Father had asked me, I think I would have recommended a lean-to built onto the south side of the barn.

I don't think I am any lazier than the next man, but I certainly approve the general idea of extended architecture. It may not meet all the aesthetic requirements of traditional and classic styles; but some of the buildings I see today don't seem to have much tradition either.

Lighting-Up Time

November was the time of year when Father wanted to get the wood cut for the next season's use, and on a Saturday afternoon as I came down the fields from the pasture woodlot, I could see the golden shafts of light slanting through the kitchen windows onto the brown, bare yard.

I can still see that row of kerosene lamps on the shelf above the sink, and I remember the fuss my sisters made when they had to wash the lamp chimneys. Several hand lamps were necessary in a family of six. We used them to light our way to bed, and sometimes I liked one near me on the red-and-white-checked cloth of the kitchen table. The sisters complained moderately about the lamps, but they could really do a first-class job on a boy who turned a barn lantern too high and allowed black soot to streak the inside of the globe. It was more of a job to wash the lantern globes because they had to be removed from the strong wire frame which protected them.

It was a big event on Mountain View Farm when Father decided he could afford one of the big, handsome, hanging lamps to attach to the ceiling over the kitchen table. It was very expensive, $6.85, but Father wanted his children to have every advantage for a good education.

The lamp hung on chains. It had a shining brass bowl and a center draft-burner that generated eighty-five candle light. The mail catalog was enthusiastic. "Fount and dome are beautifully decorated with hand-painted carnations. There are 30 cut-glass, sparkling pendants suspended from the dome band." Not quite so beautiful, perhaps, as the snowy porcelain globe of the parlor lamp on which Aunt Maude had painted magnificent petunias. But the hanging lamp was an important addition. It gave a generous and well-diffused light. Half a century ago boys and girls, men and women spent pleasant fall evenings in the mellow glow.

Mother and the Model T

It was a major event when Father said he guessed we could get a Model T. The apple crop was good, the mortgage had been cleared, and Mother had a new kitchen range and a parlor organ.

We bought the car in the fall as soon as the apple money came in. We knew we had just a few weeks to drive it before setting it up on blocks for the winter, but the family, meaning four children, put the pressure on Father. All of us learned to drive except Mother. With five in the family to drive, Mother said she did not intend to learn. She could still drive Old Jerry if for any reason she needed to go to the village.

I already knew how to drive from practicing with a friend whose father had bought a Model T the previous year. I taught Father and the three sisters to drive. Then Father began putting the pressure on Mother. "You don't know, Rosie, when you'll need to know how. The children might be away and you might want to drive to the Ladies' Sewing Circle or to a missionary meeting. You ought to learn. There's nothing to it, and you'll feel better if you know how."

The campaign went along for weeks. Sisters and I were on Father's side. It just seemed common sense that with a car in the family, everyone should know how to operate it. Finally Mother gave in. "All right," she said. "I'll learn how to drive the thing, but Haydn will have to teach me. If Frank does I know I'll be too nervous. Mrs. Sheldon let her husband teach her, and she told me she was so nervous that she cried."

So Mother and I began our lessons. Mother was really afraid of the car. I could sense her nervousness. We went riding together up and down the country road. I stopped and started; I showed her how to set the spark and gas levers and just where to place the crank so that one quick jerk would start the engine. "I'll never crank this thing in my life," she said. "All I want to know is how to drive it once the engine is started." I argued in vain. If she stalled the car, she would just wait until someone came along. So we concentrated on the gear pedal, the reverse and the foot brake. When the family was otherwise engaged, we practiced in the big front yard.

Came the time when Mother said she would drive to the village, and to this day I don't know why I let Father sit in front while I climbed into the back seat. I cranked up; Mother held the wheel in a tight grip. We started down the slight slope of the lawn to the road where we made a right angle turn to head to the village. We crept forward at a snail's pace. Mother's face was set; she was tense as a piano wire.

We crawled ahead, over the edge of the lawn to the road. Mother's iron grasp was on the wheel. We slowly inched across the rest of the road and came to the stone wall. We hit the wall, and stopped.

It was a gentle bump. The car stalled. For a moment there was silence. "Goodness gracious, Rosie!" Father said. Mother looked at Father; she looked at me. "I'm going back to the house," she said. "You can drive this monster."

Buttoning Up

It is time to button up the farmstead for the winter. No matter how well a man plans his schedule, it seems there are always last minute tasks before winter begins. Now that the last of the corn shocks have been hauled in and stacked on the big barn floor and now that the fall plowing is finished, the countryman goes about buttoning up for the cold months ahead.

After the first chilling dose of Squaw Winter, there is often a period of two or three weeks of mild weather. Some days are cloudy and the countryside is a pastel blend of soft grays, browns, and pewter hues. There are days when the low sun sends bright rays from a blue sky and the fences and walls, silos and corn cribs are starkly silhouetted. There are spectacular, flaming-red sunsets when the hardwoods on the ridges paint a picture against the sky.

It is a deep and satisfying feeling that the true countryman experiences as the days work on and he prepares his homestead against the elements. There are loose shingles and clapboards to be tightened, window glass to be puttied, storm windows to go on, a board in the kitchen stoop to be replaced, barn cracks to be covered, and machinery to be greased and stored.

When I was a boy, banking the house on a November Saturday was a job that I enjoyed. The oak stakes and twelve-inch-wide hemlock boards were brought down from the west scaffold; the stakes were driven into the ground and the weather-stained boards set in place. Then came the interesting part of the job—the trips to Johnson's sawmill for the necessary two or three loads of sawdust. Long before the insulating quality of wood was discovered, farmers knew that a trough full of sawdust around the house, reaching above the lowest clapboard, would effectively discourage the cold, probing fingers of winter winds.

It was always pleasant to get together with other lads who were at the mill for the same purpose. Shoveling sawdust is light and easy work compared with shoveling barnyard dressing or heavy gravel for the long farm driveway. When you returned, the trough around the house foundation had to be filled and tramped. "Unless you tramp it well, the wind will get through," Father said. We don't see sawdust-banked houses very often today; it is easy to slap up a roll of building paper. But here and there one still sees a farm home, well banked with the wooden chips, ready to keep out the chilling currents of frosty air that come down from the northland.

Another pleasant day's work is to haul down loads of pine branches for winter kindling. The garden is cleaned up and dressing spread for soil protection and to free its chemicals before the ground freezes. There is, naturally, a question as to the desirability or necessity of raking the leaves again before winter sets in. If the leaves dry out and a good gusty wind comes along, many of the leaves will be swirled away. On the other hand, if they blow into one's own hedge instead of a neighbor's, it means additional work in the spring.

Those who accept the cycles of the turning year as they come find that late fall is a good and satisfying time. With a cellar full of food, a barn full of good clover and timothy, and a woodshed heaped high, a man enjoys buttoning up for nature's time of rest.

Rising Wind

When the countryside is turning gray and brown, the voice of the rising wind is heard in the land. A man feels the increasing power as he does the fall plowing. When he goes to the pine lot for a load of dry branches for kindling, he hears the higher-pitched hum in the branches of the evergreens. On stormy days when he is puttering in the farm shop, the wind flings sleet and rain against the windows and pulsing gusts rattle the window frames.

The winds press, tug, and push on a raw, gray-brown November day, as if anxious to blow away the remaining days of the year. The dictionary often takes a prosaic, unimaginative view of many things that deserve a few colorful adjectives and adverbs. Of wind it says tersely: "air in motion with any degree of velocity." That may suffice for the technically–minded who make a career of splitting hairs, but it does not satisfy a farmer on the way to the barn at dawn when he feels the keen, biting edge of cold air against his face.

Of course, the *Almanac* and calendar insist that winter does not begin in November, but there are years when a man believes the astronomers reconsider. There are eleventh–month days when gray clouds hang low; there are days when cold rains savagely pelt the cringing land and skitters of hard snow swirl over the bleached, brown fields. A farmer hauling in his last loads of cornstalks or the stacks of yellow-eye beans turns his sheepskin collar high and pulls his cap down tightly on his head.

The winds tell us for certain that a year is ending. Gusty, tugging winds snap tree branches and whirl dark dust funnels over the fields. November wind plays solemn organ music among the leathery oak leaves on the pasture hillside. At night there's wild shouting and loud laughter in the hills; there's moaning around the house corners and cries in the chimney. When November winds work themselves to a frenzy, one is sure that the year's last chapter is nearly written.

DECEMBER

THERE ARE THOSE WHO DREAD THE YEAR'S FINAL SEGMENT. For now come the final pages of the annual account book. December is frequently a gray month as these last few days of the year slide downhill. The sun rises late and reluctantly and takes a low arc across the sky. There is often a blazing redness to a December dawn that one sees in no other month. When day is done, the sun seems to drop abruptly behind the hills, and granite peaks flame momentarily before surrendering to twelfth-month darkness.

But there is a sense of tranquility in the last month. Go out on a clear night and look toward the heavens, for when conditions are right, this is the month to see the stars. In the northern hemisphere four large planets dominate: Venus, Jupiter, Mars, and Saturn. There is something especially appealing in the glory of the stars on a frost-crisp winter night. There are those who feel that at no other time of year can they sense so powerfully the vastness of our universe.

While December is likely to be a gray month, there are days when an intense light outlines farmstead, fences and trees. Safe in their burrows, the woodchucks and chipmunks are curled in the awesome half-death of hibernation. Gray squirrels have built bulky leaf nests in the maples, and queen bumblebees are sleeping in mouse burrows or beneath logs. Beavers are anchoring food logs on the bottom of their ponds and deer are gathered in the evergreen swamps.

Perhaps the quietness of December is its most distinctive trait. In no other month of the year are there such long periods of noiselessness. As I walk the acres on a cloud-quilted day, the sound of my footsteps on the frost-brittle grass is loud. When I stand for a period on the high slope of the East Forty and look down to the village square, silence is deep. In the distance I may hear the rumbling of a car; a dog barks over on the Francestown road; in the far distance I may hear the faint high-pitched whir of a power saw.

But the feeling is one of brooding silence. Earth is waiting for its covering. We may not feel ready for winter but nature operates on schedule. Look at the small buds on the branches. In those small capsules are the leaves and fruit buds, wrapped tightly and waterproofed, waiting out the time until a new season is here. Life juices have drained from grasses, and the roots are safe in the soil that will mean another carpet of grass. Untold billions of seeds are waiting on the soil surface. The pines, hemlocks and tamaracks still hold their cones, and sometime in the coming summer, the hard scales will open and the seeds will ride away on the wind.

A countryman does not dislike December. The cold is hardening the ground. Winds come from the north and cry in the chimney. Nature's cycle is ending, but it will soon begin again.

The First Snowfall

Along in the forenoon of a gray, brooding, December day, a man can feel snow in the air. A storm is in the making. Smoke from farmhouse chimneys rises heavily and trails off southwestward. Stratus clouds thicken; dark streaks are smudged through the gray curtain that hangs low above the land. By noon the wind has freshened, the temperature has started to drop, and stratus clouds have changed to nimbus.

The earth is waiting—waiting patiently for whiteness to cover the drab brown and stained gray, waiting for the whiteness that conceals the bleached and blackened grasses and flowers. In the hushed quietness, the sound of the distant village bell is clear and sweet; the lonesome whistle of the valley train floats over waiting hills and fields. Hour by hour the waiting mood grows in intensity; hour by hour the feel of snow is more certain.

Scientists can give us the facts about snow but they can't describe how a man feels as he waits for the snow to begin. Science can't measure a man's heart and mind as the first large flakes begin floating casually earthward. For an hour the unhurried introduction continues; then the storm increases its tempo and the flakes begin to fall thickly. Early dusk hides the hills and the storm settles in for the night. When light returns to the world in the morning, there is a blanket of white on upland fields and lowland meadows, and when the sun breaks through in midmorning, there is white beauty on the land.

It is a fresh, sparkling world. The deciduous trees are black-and-white prints with lines of white on the limbs; the evergreens wear ermine capes and the patches of snow against the green needles make a spectacular picture in the sunlight. The old stone walls are black-and-white chains around the fields and hillside pastures. The fence posts wear jaunty white stocking caps. Down in the garden the wire pea trellis is a sparkling geometric pattern, and the hay-covered rows of strawberries are long mounds of soft cotton.

As the sun rises above the evergreens to the southeast of the big field, its slanting rays gleam in the crystals of snow. The best place to see the glowing colors is on a sidehill that rises to the north or west, just as the sun starts its winter-day journey. In the magic of early daylight you can see a wide range of colors: reds and maroons, purples and blues, wines and ambers, and glints of gold. The hillside pasture is dotted with boulders and an occasional gray beech that stands in majesty above the birches and sumacs. If a wind springs up, patches of grass and hardhack begin to show around the rocks. Here and there you can see the dainty tracks of field mice where they have hunted for grass seeds. Along the pasture wall where nearly a century ago a man set out a few apple trees you can see where a deer pawed the snow to get at the fallen fruit. Pheasants have dug into the wizened apples for the black seeds. There may be bits of bark and buds scattered on the snow left by the partridges that breakfasted on the fruit buds.

From a hilltop on a clear December day when new snow has covered the countryside, you can see a white world of incredible beauty. In the valley below, the line of the river is marked by a row of willows. Up and down the valley road, the sets of farm buildings are a picture-postcard scene, a scene that you will carry in your heart for many months to come.

The Chickadee

There is something about the cheerful, hardy, little black-cap that appeals to most persons. No matter how cold the weather, how gusty the wind or how deep the snow, the small bird sounds his optimistic "chick-a-dee-dee-dee" as he comes to the kitchen window feeder. When summer birds leave for the southland, black-cap comes from the woodlands and spends time each day around the farmstead.

In early spring, the chickadees go to the woods and build their nests in decayed limbs and tree trunks. The nests are lined with plant fibers, ferns and feathers. Often there are six to eight, occasionally ten, tiny, white eggs with purple-reddish spots. The helpful male does his part in nest building, takes his turn at incubating, and labors faithfully at feeding the little ones. Now in December the chickadees are settled into their winter routine. Hibernating insects and insect eggs are staple foods for them, and authorities tell us they are one of the most valuable species of birds in checking insect pests.

I do not know why these small, blithe-spirited birds spend the winter in the cold northland when larger birds leave for an easier climate. But I am glad that they choose to stay. In their conservative gray-and-black cloaks that blend with the winter landscape and in their cheery, friendly notes, the chickadees are a source of enjoyment and reassurance as winter's cold months work by.

Skating Party

Norway Pond in Hancock is a blue jewel in summer in a setting of green fields and woods. In winter, depending on the snow, it is either an icy diamond flashing in the sun, or it is a smooth white blanket.

A teen-ager half a century ago was undecided about which he preferred. The farmers and villagers wanted the ice, for the ice harvest was important in the days when ice was needed for iceboxes and for milk troughs. But boys who liked the thrill of steering a double runner down the steep hill roads liked both skating and sliding.

On a moonlight night, when the ice was smooth and thick, boys and girls, and sometimes older folks, began to gather at the pond. Boys went into the woods along the east bank and pulled out dead branches for the fire, for somehow a party wasn't complete without a bonfire at the shore edge. Usually the older teenagers exerted their authority over twelve-year-olds and made them gather the fuel.

Twelve- and fourteen-year-olds were scornful of the older boys who seemed to find enjoyment holding hands with a girl while skating. But some of the couples put on displays of skating that were graceful ballets. Sometimes we snapped the whip with a long line of boys holding firmly to each other, and the lad at the end of the line getting a breath-taking snap. Sometimes we had a hockey game at one end of the pond.

There is something about skating that is different from other sports. I mean the skating when one feels the bite of sharp edges in the ice, the wonderful sense of freedom and control as one speeds straight away, turns in circles, or comes to a sudden stop with ice shavings flying into the air from the skates' edges. "Free as a bird" is an expression I have heard from boyhood days, and it may be that part of the appeal in skating is that exhilarating feeling one has as he skims over the ice. I hope there will always be ice for those who want to enjoy skating on a moonlit night with a bonfire making a picture by the shore.

Flailing Beans

On a cold, windy Saturday in the twelfth month, a lad could be reasonably certain that Father would decide to flail the beans. A generation and more ago, thrifty countrymen grew their own prized strains of red kidneys, cranberry reds, yellow-eyes, white China, black turtle soup and Jacob's cattle. "Light soil for good-flavored beans" was an accepted axiom of the countryside. Some farmers made a practice of planting a couple of beans in each hill of field corn; some preferred to grow their Saturday night suppers and Sunday morning breakfasts in a plot by themselves.

After the first killing frost in early October, the beans were stacked around stubby birch poles, and allowed to dry out during a few sunny days and frosty, starlit nights. Later the bulky bundles of brittle leaves and withered pods were stacked under the west scaffold of the horse barn until a windy day in December. Then the big barn floor was swept, about a ten-inch-deep layer of pods was spread evenly over the gray planks; and we were ready for the flailing.

Flailing beans seems a simple process to the uninitiated, but there is an art to it—just as there is in mowing with a scythe or chopping with an ax. Many a lad has given himself a painful bump on the head before he has learned to swing his flail with rhythmic effectiveness. At each thump of the flail, pods burst and beans popped high in the air. After the area was flailed over, it was fluffed up with a pitchfork and the process repeated. Then the broken brittle vines were tossed aside; beans, chaff, bits of pods were swept into a big pile with a homemade birch broom. The other big barn door was opened so a strong draft would sweep through as the mixture was winnowed. From one tin tub to another the material was poured. During each pouring the wind swept away debris and eventually one had a tub of clean, colorful nuggets. The cleaned beans were stored in wooden buckets beneath the bottom shelf of the pantry. When the last wooden bucket was filled and in place Father always said, "There, I guess we will have enough Saturday suppers for another year."

One-Hole Corn Sheller

On family farms at the beginning of the century, a fourteen-year-old had a daily task as soon as he returned from District School, changed into his chore clothes, and had a lunch of

Mother's sugar cookies and a glass or two of milk. The Perfection One-Hole Corn Sheller assured the daily need of shelled corn for the livestock. It also assured a lad of exercise! A husked cob of corn went into the hole in the top; muscle power turned the iron crank that rotated the gears. The shelled cob popped out a hole at the rear, and the shelled corn dribbled into a battered tin tub beneath the machine.

The catalog description, a boy often felt, was unduly enthusiastic, especially the statement that "A bushel of corn can be shelled in this machine in five minutes." One did not question that the sheller was "strong and durable, guaranteed to give perfect satisfaction and do good work." However, as one poked a cob into the hole and started the cranking, he wondered a bit about the statement, "This sheller is supplied with a heavy balance wheel and is geared low so that it is easy to operate."

A young citizen tried once or twice to shell a bushel of corn in the five minutes mentioned, but was easily convinced that this time limit was for Paul Bunyan. The one-hole sheller served its purpose well in the days before corn raising was mechanized and the magic of hybridization increased the harvest. Not so long ago fifty bushels per acre was considered excellent yield; today one hundred bushels is commonplace and it is only a question of time until two hundred bushels will be an everyday goal.

We would not return to one-hole corn shellers any more than we would ask for a renaissance of bootjacks and buffalo robes. But the countryman feels that men who can recall the afternoon task of corn shelling have an appreciation for country life that today's boys will never have.

Train Whistle

Do you remember the train whistles? Remember the far-carrying, lonesome sound of the whistles in the days when steam engines came puffing and clattering into the small villages?

Train whistles have sounded far across the level prairies; they have sent their messages along fertile river valleys; their lonesome, high-pitched whoo-whoo-who-who has echoed among hills and mountains.

There was something familiar and yet strangely mysterious about the long-drawn call in the darkness of night as the train rushed along like a jeweled snake. Men and boys have gathered in small gray depots across the nation to wait for a train to come in with its milk jugs and egg crates, and the thin sound of the whistle far down the line was pleasant to hear.

A train whistle is primarily a practical thing. It blows for crossings in the countryside and to herald the train's arrival at a depot. But before the era of the diesel with its brassy, raucous blast, a train whistle was more than a utilitarian warning. It spoke of the conquest of frontiers; it told of mountain passes and vast plains compassed by man.

Soon there will be no more whistles from steam engines. But there are those who can remember the days before our rubber-tired era, when the train whistle, echoing across the fields and hills, was a part of American history.

The Lamplighter

For many years, lamplighters made their daily rounds in villages and towns. Old Ben was the lamplighter in our town. He was a humble, elderly man who performed his job with unfailing regularity. Each afternoon he pushed his battered old wheelbarrow along the street loaded with a stubby ladder, can of coal oil, and a bunch of greasy-looking, cleaning cloths.

Mothers and fathers never worried when their small boys followed Old Ben on his rounds. Old Ben was a character. He had been around the world on tramp steamers; he knew about fascinating far-off places and the names he used as he told stories to the small fry brought to life the material in dog-eared geography books in school. He described the wonders of far-off China and the dangers of Cape Horn. He had been to Alaska and had spent winters in the lumber camps of the Northwest.

Old Ben worked as he talked. He set up the ladder, opened the iron-frame lamp cage, took off the chimney, polished it, and refilled the lamp's reservoir. Not very exciting in this era of scientific marvels. Just an old man living out his years and earning a few needed dollars. But there are boys now sleeping the long sleep in distant lands who knew Old Ben. There are men living in teeming cities who look out office windows these winter afternoons and think of the days of long ago when they followed the lamplighter along the village street.

No one knows how or when it was learned that a dish of oil with a protruding wick would provide a steady light. Archaeologists tell us that ancient man molded rude clay vessels in the shape of animals' skulls to use for lamps. Eventually man learned to enclose the flame; in time he devised a wick that could be turned up and down and he built a closed container to hold the oil.

Man's history could be written in terms of the artificial light he has used over the centuries. When that history is written, a meaningful part will be the role played in past generations by the humble kerosene lantern. Lanterns have hung from the spars of wooden ships as they cut a course through unknown seas. Lanterns have gone with men across mountains and grasslands; they have marked the steel lines of railroads pushing across plains and valleys and through mountain passes.

Millions of men and women now living in cities remember the lantern that hung beneath the farm wagon or was attached to the dashboards of democrat wagons and pungs as families went to the village to do the Saturday evening trading. On many a lonely road, farm families have watched for the glow of the lantern marking the return of a loved one; or perhaps in an emergency have watched for the golden gleam in the darkness that meant the doctor was coming. It is part of our nation's history that when the thirteen colonies were struggling for their rights, two lanterns hung in a Boston church steeple lighted a new concept in man's upward struggle. Even today, there are still many farm and country homes where lanterns are a part of daily living.

Saturday Night Trading

Time was when Saturday evening was a highlight of the week. Farm families did the chores early, ate supper, and readied for the trip to town. Eggs and butter were packed in firkins; a bushel of handsome Northern Spies and a bushel of smooth Irish

Cobblers went under the pung's seats.

Sleigh bells jingled as fast roaders whisked along country roads and runners squeaked on the hard-packed snow. In front of the general store, Belle was snugly blanketed and the whole family trooped in. Mother bartered the farm produce for needed groceries. Father looked over the hardware counter and talked with the men around the big, potbellied, iron stove. Womenfolk gathered by the notions counter and discussed percales and ginghams, laces, hair ribbons, and apron material. A lad with a whole nickel pondered possible purchases in front of the curved glass candy counter.

Saturday night was trading night, but it was more than that too. The general store was a part of the town's social life. Men and women from farms had a chance to get the news and gossip; plans were made for socials and town suppers. And if a family was in trouble quiet-voiced men made arrangements for a chopping bee or a schedule for caring for a neighbor's stock.

Life ran at a slower tempo, and by today's standards it seems old-fashioned. But there was a special pleasure and excitement in the days of yesteryear when Saturday night trading was a part of country living.

The White Lady

The white birch is a gracious, serene lady of the woodland family. Not so common as its humbler cousin, the gray, the white birch adds appealing beauty to hillsides and mountain shoulders, to open woodlands and highland pastures.

The white birch is possibly the best known of all our trees. Against a dark background of evergreens its white beauty attracts the eye. School children are taught that the Indians used its bark for canoes. Few, however, know that the early settlers often used sheets of birch bark for house insulation.

The birch is usually an outrider of the forest. Eons ago there were vast stands of birches on the northland tundras, and in the pressing, never-ceasing winds of the northland, remarkable elasticity was built into their cells.

The bark and wood have served man well. Trappers and woodsmen favor the bark to start their fires; the close-grained, hard wood is used for spools and shoe pegs and fuel. In decades past, housewives wanted some split birch available for quick, supper fires in hot weather.

There are not too many "white ladies" left today, for man has used them ruthlessly for his needs. But here and there one sees them on the hillsides, in the woodlands and along peaceful country roads. They bow before the tempest's power; they accept their coatings of snow and sleet and when the time of travail is done, they calmly lift themselves again. Serene, dignified and gracious, they add their touch of beauty to the countryside.

Kindling for Winter

Getting ready the winter's supply of kindling was an important matter for good countrymen a generation ago. One could stoke the parlor burner with solid, knotty chunks of maple, oak, ash and hickory in the evening so there would be a bed of coals ready for kindling in the morning. It meant the living-room was warm, and a fellow could take his clothes from a cold bedroom and dress by the stove. The cold kitchen was a different story. A man wanted plenty of quick-catching kindling and the right kinds of wood to get a hot fire going quickly.

This quotation is from the *New England Farmer*, in 1857. "These cold December mornings, making a fire is a very necessary domestic item, and to do it certainly and quickly will save growls and whines. Not only will it prove a saving of passion, but a saving of pence; for as usually happens, the right way is the cheapest way in the end. What life it would infuse, how perfectly it would wake up a lazy sleeping child, if compelled to bounce out of bed at daylight of a winter's morning and light the fire. It sends the lazy sleeping blood to the remotest extremities, and quickens the body. It vitalizes the man."

Could be, of course, although the children in my life seldom bounced out of bed. Furthermore, a cold kitchen doesn't necessarily send the blood racing to one's extremities. A man accepts the job of building the fire, but on pleasant, mild December days, he gets up his winter's kindling supply. On a good day, he hitches up his horse and goes to the pine woodlot for several loads of the dry, dead branches which he knocks from the trunks. Citizens differ in their opinions concerning the merits of various kindling materials, but after forty years of objective experiment, the countryman prefers short pieces of small-diameter, resin-filled pine wood. Getting the kindling for winter is a routine, unpretentious task, but when night comes and a man looks at the pile of dry limbs ready to be chopped on a stormy day, it means that another task of getting ready for winter has been finished.

Kitchen Rocking Chair

When a man comes in from afternoon chores, it is good to have a rocking chair available in the kitchen. The milking is done; cows and horses are bedded down; pigs and chickens fed. The woodbox by the wood-burning range is heaped with solid dry oak, maple, and ash, and the kindling box has plenty of dry pine and finely-split gray birch to start the fire come tomorrow's cold morning. I am not opposed to the new-fangled chairs that lower a man's head and elevate his feet, but nothing to date offers quite the degree of comfort, soothing motion, and a sense of all's right with the world as an old-fashioned rocker.

I wish every man had the chance to relax after supper in a kitchen rocker with his socked feet in the open oven of a wood or coal-burning kitchen stove. That is genuine radiant heat, and in its radiance a man can read, talk, and snooze comfortably through quiet winter evenings. There is nothing to equal the heat from an old-fashioned stove with a porcelain-lined water tank on the rear and a warming oven above. The baking oven is meant to hold a man's feet. In the golden glow of a kerosene lamp, you can read the farm journals as you listen to the teakettle sing on the stove. In the course of each day's living, every one needs the opportunity to recharge drained batteries, and no environment is better than a comfortable rocker before an open oven.

Feather Beds

In earlier times the four-poster was the most important piece of furniture in the one-room cabin, important enough so that it often headed the list of articles in wills. The old-time feather bed was a completely homemade affair. The bed frame, made of maple, ash or oak, was corded with hemp spun by the farmer's wife and washed, pulled and twisted into a strong rope. That was what I had as a boy in the small room beneath the eaves of the old farmhouse. The rope was laced lengthwise and crosswise, pulled taut. Over the rope foundation we put what Mother called the underbed. This was made of heavy ticking and filled with clean oat straw or corn husks. The ticking was homemade of flax, which was grown, processed, and spun on the farm.

Then over the underbed came the feather bed proper. In the pleasant, unhurried days of buffalo robes and homemade bread, housewives were proud of the fluffy affairs. Goose feathers, according to Grandmother, were by far the best filling, but half a century ago goose raising was on the way out, so hen feathers were used on most farms. Sometimes the feathers of wild turkeys or ducks were also used.

Long-ago diaries and journals tell of bed ticks filled with wild pigeons' feathers. Pigeons, literally by the millions, flew sky trails in certain areas, and came to roost and feed in vast beech forests. There they could be caught with a slip and a noose.

Each spring good housewives put the feather mattresses over outdoor clotheslines to air and sun. Occasionally a housewife decided to wash and dry the feathers, and there are men and women today who can remember stirring the feathers in tubs and buckets as the feathers dried on a sunny, windless day.

On cold winter nights I would like once more to see a feather bed waiting, fluffed high, with three soapstones warming strategic spots. Give a man a first-class feather bed, a few cotton blankets, a couple of homemade quilts, and a flannel nightgown long enough to wrap around his toes, and he can enjoy a good night's sleep.

December Sunset

The sun climbs a low arc from southeast to southwest across a cloudless, pale blue sky. Brilliant, slanting rays light the countryside like a powerful searchlight. Walls and fences are stark lines on a faded landscape; silos stand tall against the sky and the mountains across the valley are sharply etched against the horizon.

On such a day, there is often a spectacular sunset. Just before the sun disappears, glowing colors climb suddenly into the sky. If atmospheric conditions are right, December sunset is painted with deep, soft reds, rich saffrons, and broad streaks of pale blue. Sometimes the colors form a gigantic, smooth-edged circle; sometimes the colors flame in triangles. The colors in the sky are briefly reflected on the landscape and transform gray-brown fields and meadows, pastures and sidehills into a soft-hued, amber-tinted panorama.

For a few poignant minutes the colors bless the land. Then, quickly the colors fade. Against the western sky, bare-limbed trees are sharply silhouetted; dark shadows gather in the valleys and night's curtain drops abruptly. Lights shine from kitchen windows; stars break through; and the quiet of year's end falls over the December landscape.

Christmas

Do you remember Christmas before it became a Chamber of Commerce spectacular? In the days when oranges were a treat instead of a source of Vitamin C, my sisters and I began preparations for Christmas well ahead. Now let me answer a question that has often been raised concerning my holiday spirit. If you were the only boy in a family with three girls, wouldn't you do a little calculating?

I do not pretend to remember the gifts that we found on Christmas morning. I know that we hung our long stockings from the mantel behind the tall base-burner in the living room. I know that for many years each of us was certain to find a shiny dime, an orange, and a bag of candy when we came downstairs. What I remember is something deeper and something richer. One of the memories is the afternoon of the day before Christmas when Father and I took a hand ax, and together climbed the orchard slope and went into the evergreen grove beyond the apple trees.

For years getting the Christmas tree was an annual ritual. It was a leisurely expedition and we took our time in walking the woodland and searching for just the right tree. Father wanted a tree about seven feet high—a spruce with evenly balanced limbs and a strong top spike.

The evergreen woodland in December was a peaceful sanctuary. Some years the snow had come and the Temple Mountains across the Contoocook Valley were sparkling in the slanting rays. Some years it was a gray, quiet day with the countryside brooding in the hushed waiting period before the snow.

I remember how we trimmed the Christmas tree after supper on Christmas Eve. Probably it would be more accurate to say that Mother and sisters trimmed the tree. I can still see those shoe boxes of ornaments. All year long they sat on the top shelf of the front hall closet. There were long strands of silvery tinsel, fragile, red balls, and red paper bells that folded like accordions. During the day, my sisters made long strings of red cranberries and strands of white popcorn. I can see the brown gingerbread men that Mother made—always four of them so each of us could have one. Then Father stood on a chair and fastened the big, gleaming, white star to the top spike. When all the trimmings were on, we brought our presents from their hiding places. The bigger parcels went on the floor beneath the branches; smaller packages were placed among the upper branches.

When the tree was trimmed and all the presents ready for Christmas morning, Father took his well-worn Bible, and while we listened he read again the old, but ever-new and thrilling story of the Wise Men who followed a guiding star and came to the Babe in the Manger. That, I think, is what I remember best over the years. It would not have been Christmas without the story. And when a lad took his lamp and climbed the steep stairs to his room, he remembered Father's words. "Some day, somehow, men will learn to live in peace and goodwill." The years are many and the years are long. But a grown man remembers those words. Some day, somehow, all men will be brothers. That must be our hope, for there is no other way.